SOLAR CONSCIENCE
LUNAR CONSCIENCE

SOLAR CONSCIENCE
LUNAR CONSCIENCE

An Essay on the Psychological Foundations
of Morality, Lawfulness, and
the Sense of Justice

Murray Stein

Chiron Publications ◆ Wilmette, Illinois

Library of Congress Catalog Card Number: 93-11414

Printed in the United States of America.
Editing and book design by Siobhan Drummond.
Cover design by D. J. Hyde.

Library of Congress Cataloging-in-Publication Data:
Stein, Murray, 1943-
  Solar conscience, lunar conscience : an essay on the
psychological foundations of morality, lawfulness, and the sense of
justice / Murray Stein.
      p.   cm.
  Includes bibliographical references and index.
  ISBN 0-933029-72-1 : $14.95
  1. Conscience. 2. Ethics--Psychological aspects. 3. Mythology,
Greek--Psychological aspects. 4. Jung, C. G. (Carl Gustav), 1875-
1961. I. Title.
BJ1471.S685 1993
170--dc20   93-11414
                                                   CIP

CONTENTS

PREFACE

Søren Kierkegaard's *Purity of Heart Is to Will One Thing* fell into my hands when I was twenty years old. I had found a paperback English translation of it on sale in a bin of used books outside a bookshop in Paris during summer vacation between my junior and senior years in college. I was traveling alone, seeing Europe for the first time, and, being without a great deal of money was not seduced by the sensuous pleasures of the Parisian world. *Purity of Heart* became one of the two or three most important books of my life.

Kierkegaard went right to my center like a laser beam and illuminated a core of selfhood that had lain hidden and dormant until then. This core of selfhood has been one of my most precious treasures, the guiding compass for thousands of judgments and decisions. I have never forgotten the experience of discovering this core—it was as though I had "just emerged from a dense cloud," to use Jung's phrase for the same type of experience (Jung 1961, p. 32)—and its importance remains undiminished by time.

I felt myself become the individual to whom Kierkegaard was speaking, and in this stirring to life in the center of my being I realized for the first time consciously what I now call conscience. For me conscience is much more than the internalized pressure of parents and society to conform to certain arbitrary norms. It is importantly influenced and shaped by culture and society, as we shall see in these explorations, but its roots lie much deeper and its meaning is more transcendent and fateful.

Like Freud, I see conscience (which he called superego) as a psychological agency that exists outside the ego; but unlike Freud and rather more like Jung, I see it as a divine spark within each human. It is the voice of God, in a sense, and the inner ground for perceptions and feelings about law and justice, but it is complicated by a number of factors which I will attempt to elucidate in the following essay. It speaks ultimately, I believe, for what Jung called the Self, and like the Self it is a complexity. The voice of conscience transcends social pressure and custom. If it did not, how would we have prophets and moral, creative geniuses like Albert Schweitzer, Gandhi, and Simone Weil, who rise above the mores of their times and criticize them? Like science, with its Newtons and Einsteins, the moral world has its geniuses, too, and their intelligence is no less acute and penetrating, even though it is guided by the value of justice rather than by mathematical intuitions and formulas.

Several years after finding Kierkegaard's book in Paris I came upon Jung's autobiography, *Memories, Dreams, Reflections.* This is the second in that small group of books that have transformed my life. For me this singular account of a life bore eloquent testimony to Kierkegaard's intuitions in *Purity of Heart.* The one thing that Jung willed, as recorded in his autobiography by himself and Aniela Jaffe, was a life of wholeness and integrity. The notion that wholeness is the one thing worth willing with all one's passion added the necessary psychological ingredient to Kierkegaard's more philosophical and theological formulations. Jung grounded the passion for selfhood and integrity and justice in real life and in everyday existence. This became my guiding thread in writing the essay that follows.

I want to thank my friends Nathan Schwartz-Salant and John Beebe for their encouragement in publishing this book. I would like to acknowledge, too, the enormous debt of gratitude I feel for my Zurich analysts, Dr. Hilde Binswanger and Dr. Richard Pope, with whom I was allowed to experience the psyche to whatever depth I was capable at the time. Many of my first insights and ideas about conscience came through that work, and while the years since then have brought refinements and further elaborations, the basic context for this discussion was created in those analytic experiences.

I have tried to steer clear of philosophy and theology in these pages. The literature on ethics and moral development is vast. My own interest lies in the emotional and psychological side of the issue, in our "gut reactions" about right and wrong, good and evil. I also wanted to make these reflections on conscience accessible to the general reader while still hoping that they make a contribution to the field of depth psychology.

My wife Jan has been a long-standing conversation partner on all the contents of this work. I thank her for her astute insights and generous attitude. In many ways, she has been and still is my teacher on matters of feeling and empathy.

To Siobhan Drummond, the editor, I also owe a word of gratitude, not only for her meticulous care with the text but also for her helpful suggestions for its improvement.

Chapter One

THE COMPLEXITY OF CONSCIENCE

At the mythological heart of the American nation lies a story of conscience. As a boy, George Washington cut down a cherry tree and was confronted with the problem that,when it awakens, tortures every human conscience: to tell the truth or to lie. He refused to hide behind deception when asked about it, and rather than protect his image he spoke the famous words, "I cannot tell a lie." Every American schoolchild learns this story and is encouraged to be similarly truthful. Upon such tales rests the character of a nation.

This apocryphal story exposes the essence of conscience. George Washington did not have time to think about the pros and cons of answering the question this way or that. Nor did he consult anyone else. He responded spontaneously. Conscience is a gut reaction, and it belongs to the individual. It is not the product of rational thought and reflection. It is an inner agency that speaks for values that are not necessarily identical with the immediate self-interest of the individual. George Washington, the father of our country, is held up as a model of integrity. We are all supposed to act like he did. This image encourages the truth-teller in all of us. It supports our own conscience, an inner imperative, a still, small voice.

Conscience is a complex and far-reaching feature in the psychological life of every individual. In fact, it takes so many forms and insinuates itself into so many of our judgments and emotional reactions that the job of pinning it down and analyzing it as a single psychological factor becomes extremely difficult. In everyday life, in the media, on the streets, voices speak of "professional conscience," "social conscience," "artistic conscience," "political conscience," "personal conscience," "collective conscience," on and on. Moreover, guilt and a bad conscience can appear in apparently limitless variety. Conscience pangs strike in connection with sex, power, money, politics, food and drink, scholarship, racial attitudes, relationships, and a varied assortment of other issues and activities. Conscience seems capable of picking on any, or every, aspect of human life and behavior and producing ripples of guilt around it.

Beneath the welter of these phenomena, however, we can discover some common psychological themes and dynamics. Conscience seems always to confront a person with negative restrictions and positive demands that go against the flow of other spontaneous impulses, and these prohibitions and commands are essentially nonegotistical or even antiegotistical in character. Conscience presses us with claims that originate beyond the ego, which I will understand throughout this essay as the center of individual consciousness, the "I-ness" of a person's experience. The effect generated by these extraegoistic claims is to thwart our seemingly natural and infinitely cunning desire to base our decisions simply on "what I want right now!" Imaged as a voice, conscience urges us to sacrifice wishes, impulses, and plans for the sake of some "other," for a value, claim, or person who exists outside the area identified by the ego as the immediate sphere of self-interest.

Conscience creates a psychological state of ambivalence. But this is not the type of ambivalence that rests on simply wanting two contradictory things at once, chocolate versus vanilla ice cream; rather it is an ambivalence stemming from "I want this, but it demands that." There is an "other" in the picture. This ambivalence-creating activity of the psychic factor that we call conscience is capable of striking wherever the ego has claims and wishes of its own. For this reason, we find such a wide variety of issues falling under the rubric of "problems of conscience." Conscience rests on awareness of an "other" and on the perception that justice means taking the other into account as much as oneself.

WHAT CONSCIENCE WANTS

Undoubtedly a finely tuned conscience is one of the noblest of human endowments. It is what we admire in a George Washington, a Gandhi, or a Madame Curie. Without conscience a person is hardly recognizably human. In fact, most of us shudder and turn away when we meet up with someone who shows little evidence of conscience, a cold-blooded rapist or killer or a cheat, someone who can go on without a pang of guilt or a sign of empathy for the victim. The psychopathic personality seems like a horrible mistake of nature and a terrible failure of culture.

And yet, a too finely tuned conscience turns into neurosis. Scrupulosity, the hyperdevelopment of moral conscientiousness, has been recognized as one of the major pitfalls of religious life. It is considered a disease that carries the drive for purity and perfection to debilitating lengths. At the opposite end of the moral continuum from psychopathy, scrupulosity kills the individual under the burning gaze of a conscience too bright and too hot. No cleanliness can be exact enough, no confession complete or deep enough to remove the stain of guilt, and no motive is shadow-free and pure enough to pass the inspection of the interior grand inquisitor. It was this kind of conscience that drove Luther to distraction and self-flagellation until he discovered the meaning of divine grace and forgiveness.

At both ends of this moral spectrum we find something monstrous. The person with no conscience strikes us as inhuman; the person with too much conscience becomes an emotional cripple.

What does conscience want? What should it want? To ask this is to ask the ethical question of conscience itself.

The simple answer to the question of what conscience wants is that it wants the "right thing." It is the internal sense of right and wrong, a sort of inner psychic gyroscope that tells moral up from down and east from west. At the most basic level of experience, conscience is less the result of cognition and conscious reflection than a gut feeling, an instinctive sense and knowledge of the difference between good and evil. According to the biblical myth, we are born with a conscience because Adam and Eve sinned. They ate from the tree of the knowledge of good and evil, and we have inherited this knowledge. As refined as ethical reflection can become, and granting the several levels of ethical cognition delineated by Kohlberg (1973), the most basic and most lofty examples of conscience are still instinctive. The moral geniuses, such as Albert Schweitzer and Mahatma Gandhi, begin with and build upon an intuition of right and wrong that cognition follows, rationalizes, refines, and attempts to explain but cannot create. Conscience comes in the form of instinctive knowledge. It is a kind of gnosis.

What must be recognized about conscience is that it is a psychological factor. In all that follows, this will be the platform on which everything else rests. In this essay, I will try to situate conscience within the psychological world as described by Jung. I cannot, of course, give a full account of analytical psychology's theory here; I refer the reader to Edward C. Whitmont's *The Symbolic Quest*, Jolande Jacobi's *The Psychology of C. G. Jung*, and Elie Humbert's *C. G. Jung* for a full exposition. For now, it must suffice to say that this is a psychological universe in which the term *Self* refers to the whole of a person, inclusive of conscious and unconscious aspects of the psyche as well as somatic and spiritual elements. Terms like *ego, complex,* and *archetype* refer to parts of that wholeness. The ego is the "I," the locus of personal identity, within this psychological universe, while the complexes are autonomous pieces of personality that exist as residues of personal history and experience, and the archetypes are autonomous pieces ("patterns of behavior and perception") that are impersonal and inherited as genetic structure.

CONSCIENCE AS A VOICE FOR THE INNER OTHER

Conscience manifests itself as a nonegoistic attitude that treats one's own ego more or less as it would another person. Conscience does not recognize the ego as a privileged figure in the psychic world. What conscience demands and presses toward is not necessarily "my good," in the narrow sense, but "the good" in a broader, less personal sense. It refuses to consider the ego complex as a special case or to grant it unique rights and prerogatives. From the viewpoint of conscience, egotism is tantamount to evil, and the ego's claim to absolute supremacy over the other contents of the psyche and over other people is likewise evil. Conscience says that we should not try to make ourselves too special.

This by itself is not enough to establish the claim that conscience has its seat outside the ego. It could be a minority position within the ego. In that case, though, the ego would have relatively strong control over conscience. What is most telling is that conscience cannot be brought definitively under control of the ego. It behaves like an autonomous complex. To a certain extent, the ego can master the effects of complexes in the short run, but it cannot become their master in the long run.

One of the ego's typical grandiose illusions is that it is in control of the psyche and can dominate the other complexes in the psychic household. This was the premise of Raskolnikov in Dostoevsky's *Crime and Punishment*. He murders the old woman Alyona Ivanovna, robs her, and assumes he will be able to manipulate his psychic reactions to this crime. His experiment fails utterly, and he discovers that his conscience is far more powerful than he recognized. This brilliant psychological novel exposes the ego's naïveté about conscience. Conscience is a daimon, a mighty force that the ego cannot monopolize, and it determines a person's fate far beyond what we may think of as free will.

How conscience works its will and how it is inwardly structured form the major concerns of this essay, for its ways are numerous, some blatant but many subtle. Its freedom from the ego's domination means that it is rooted in another psychological place apart. In depth psychology parlance, we might speak of a "conscience complex," but as our insight into its workings and structures deepens, we will see that it is more archetypal than personal, deeper, bigger, and more important than what we usually dismiss as a mere "complex." Unlike the complex, conscience does not have its inevitable origin in a trauma; rather it comes with the species, so to speak. Its presence is innately human. It is a universal human given, although its specific content may be vastly different from culture to culture.

We will see, too, that like all archetypal factors, conscience is itself a complexity and contains polarities. Conscience is, as it were, a pair of pincers that can affect a person's life from right or left, from conscious and unconscious, from mind as well as body. But in whatever form it appears or with whatever voice it speaks, its thrust and message seem always to be aimed at correcting a narrowly egoistical attitude, that is, an attitude based too narrowly on what a person perceives consciously or half-consciously to be pure self-interest.

One of the important contributions that Jungian analytical psychology has made to the understanding of conscience is in realizing it can also speak for the so-called "inner world" of complexes and archetypes. The more conventional view of conscience sees it as representing the demands, norms, and ideals of a society, a tradition, or a religion. The "other" is always reduced to brothers and sisters, our fellow citizens, or to the more abstract rules and regulations promulgated by authorities in the environment. Conscience is seen as an internal spokesperson for social values.

While conscience does indeed often speak in this fashion for the rights of others and in behalf of their suffering and needs, it also can take up the rights and needs of one's own neglected and unlived emotional life. To take up for unlived life might be a form of self-interest in a broader sense of that term, but it certainly does not feel immediately like self-interest. While conscience often seems to humble the ego in favor of the group, it also does so for the sake of the neglected child within, the repressed shadow, and the starving anima or animus. Conscience can demand that we attend to unlived life and perhaps even live it out, as untoward and distasteful as this may be.

What this indicates is that conscience is also independent of group pressure and its collective agendas, conscious and unconscious. What has made conscience so suspect to totalitarian groups, and especially to their leaders, stems precisely from this: it is able to impose upon the ego an inwardly determined point of view and make demands contrary to what external authority may dictate. The group, which is held together by collective adherence to a dominant pattern of thought or to specific leaders and their values and behavior, cannot control an individual's conscience. This is what made Aleksandr Solzhenitsyn and his writings such a threat in Soviet Russia. The fate of persons like Solzhenitsyn was one of the chief anguishes within the late Soviet system. These people spoke for conscience against the enforced collective values of the state. They could not be silenced.

For the individual who experiences conscience as this inward voice of personhood which comes into conflict with collective values and attitudes, there are also enormous difficulties. How is one to know that conscience speaks the truth? How can one be certain that this is not simply inflation and grandiosity? Having learned the conventions of collective life, a person can be thrown into dreadful conflict by the contrary view of a conscience that speaks for the hidden and denied needs of the soul. This is the dilemma of a Luther, of a Gandhi, of a Sakharov. In their bellies, these people know something is wrong, but can they be sure of the validity of their perception? How can an individual question a whole tradition or a convinced collective? An acute conflict springs up between social pressure, duty to religion, loyalty to society and culture on the one hand and the unyielding demands for life, liberty, and justice for the individual soul on the other. Perhaps it is such turbulent crises that religions seek to spare their devotees when they counsel that the tradition knows best. The voice of conscience may at times be hard to distinguish from the wily tempter, Satan himself! St. Anthony, struggling resolutely in the desert against swarms of voluptuous temptresses, was sure that the Devil had his eye on his soul, but perhaps it was his anima clamoring for justice?

CONSCIENCE AS PLURALISTIC

Conscience demands, ultimately, that all the gods be served; but from a single tradition's viewpoint, this raises many problems and conflicts. The monotheisms especially are not happy with this perspective. Each advocates absolute dedication to its version of the ultimate Power in the universe. Dedicated service to one of the psychic gods invariably casts the remaining ones in the role of devils and tempters. According to conscience, however, the real devil, genuine evil, is the ego's drive for unconditional independence and control and its love of power. Any particular attitude, religious conviction, or position may conceal the devilish tail of Satan beneath its surface if, in exchange for one-sided and exclusive service, it offers the ego the authority, power, and sense of moral righteousness it so eagerly desires. This is, for example, the temptation of the Popes, which is why they must retain a private confessor, and of analysts, which is why they retain an analyst of their own.

The classical story of Hippolytus illustrates this pluralistic principle within conscience. Hippolytus is steadfastly faithful to the virgin goddess Artemis. He is an ardent devotee. His breast swells with feelings of rectitude and uprightness as he heaps offerings and says prayers at the shrine of his favorite goddess, as he lights sacrifices in her name, as he steadfastly denies her polar opposite, the love goddess Aphrodite, even a nod of recognition. In the end, Aphrodite arranges for his destruction and brings him to grief for his pride, and Artemis is unable to protect her acolyte.

To explain why she failed to preserve Hippolytus, Artemis refers to a law that rules the Olympians:

> This is the settled custom of the Gods: No one may fly
> in the face of another's wish; we remain aloof and neu-

9

tral. Else, I assure you, had I not feared Zeus, I never would have endured such shame as this—my best friend among men killed, and I could do nothing. (Euripides *Hippolytus* 1328–1333)

Olympian law holds Artemis in check while allowing Aphrodite to exact alarming revenge: Hippolytus is lured to incest and commits suicide.

When all the psychological gods and goddesses have spoken and each has been given a voice through conscience, what is heard is the demand for wholeness and completeness rather than one-sided and narrowly defined perfection. Conscience does not seem to have a singular moral lens but a pluralistic one. While purity of heart may be to will one thing, as Kierkegaard said, that one thing is wholeness.

TWO LEVELS OF CONSCIENCE

The accounts and explanations of conscience can be roughly divided into two general positions, each of which has several versions:

1. Conscience consists of the introjected values and moral norms of society (the social-psychological view), and the driving force behind conscience is the ego's aggression toward authority figures which has been turned back upon the ego (a psychoanalytic view).

2. Conscience is the voice of God or of the gods (the religious view), and its content derives from nature or from nature's ruler(s) and may therefore shift about in a seemingly arbitrary and irrational fashion (from the human point of view).

The first explanation is reductive and psychosociological; the second is spiritual and transcendental.

Freud gave the first view what has, in modern times, become its classical expression. For Freud, conscience, which he termed the superego, comes into being as a psychic entity through identification with a figure of authority (typically the father) and through the subsequent internalization of this authority's values and standpoint. The superego gains a good deal of energy from the fear a person feels toward that authority ("castration anxiety"). Also, the aggression one feels against the authority, usually as a part of the oedipal conflict, becomes absorbed in the superego and from there is deflected back against the ego itself. Conscience is seen here as a kind of focal point of aggression against parental authority, and the stronger the aggression the harsher the conscience would be. This would explain scrupulosity as an excess of aggression against authority figures such as father, mother, priest, or bishop. As the superego expands to include more and more authority figures, the net result is a conscience that tends to coincide with many or most collective social norms.

The view that conscience results from identification with figures of authority and the introjection of them—and with them, of course, too, the introjection of collective attitudes—became nearly axiomatic in the modernist intellectual world. This led to a further extension on the part of some Freudian intellectuals like Norman O. Brown (*Love's Body*), who advocated overthrowing the oedipal tyranny of the superego and returning to the preoedipal garden of polymorphous perversion. It could be argued that the post-modernist world has indeed entered a preoedipal state in which the stringencies of the cultural superego have been abandoned in favor of the pleasures of eclecticism.

But Freud himself probably would have shunned this direction. For him it would have been inconceivable to shed the superego. Not only would this not be particularly desirable, but it would be psychologically impossible. For Freud, the superego is not only a purely personal acquisition, but it has a "phylogenetic" basis. Freud came up with the phylogenetic model in order to explain the universality of the superego, and this brought him close to an archetypal theory much like what Jung would propose, but with a curiously historical point of reference.

The expectation of punishment that the superego inflicts on the ego, Freud proposed, can be traced to a primordial memory that reaches back to the days of a primal herd. In this primal herd, Freud imagined, the father was extremely brutal and selfish, and he kept all the females for himself and denied his sons any sexual gratification. So the sons rose up and murdered him. Theirs was a Pyrrhic victory, however, for although they overcame their father and freed the female population for their own enjoyment, they had been psychologically attached to their father and so they fell into remorse for what they had done. Aggression against the father had resulted in murder, but then identification with the father meant that they felt a grievous loss and also remorse, and so their original aggression became deflected back against themselves. This moment created a permanent human psychological structure, the groundwork for the superego. The energy that drives the superego is aggression turned back against the self.

Freud's phylogenetic model deepens a purely personalistic view of conscience and its origins considerably and seems much more capable of accounting for the universality and psychic force of conscience. It also explains the extra-egoic location of conscience in the psychic world. Because of its emphasis on the image of the father, and because the content of the superego is made up of social rules and norms, it represents what I will call throughout the rest of this essay "solar conscience." Solar conscience is rooted in and backed by paternal authority. It is patriarchal conscience.

The function of the solar aspect of conscience is to press the ego into the service of collective norms, ideals, and values. The values that solar conscience espouses and the actions it recommends to the ego possess a quality of steadiness and permanence, and it seeks to maintain the status quo of particular psychological and social patterns. Solar conscience is not particularly creative. This side of conscience is more or less fully available to consciousness, and it exists in the light, so to speak. Its values and injunctions can be confirmed by others and by reference to texts. It is *con science,* "knowing with."

One finds another perspective on conscience alluded to in Jung's work. For Jung, conscience is the moral pressure of the archetypes and so is more like the voice of God than like social pressure (Jung 1958). This does not allow one to reduce conscience to something definite and clearly known within collective consciousness or applicable across the board to one and all as with solar conscience. Rather, Jung points to an at least partially irrational, unknowable, shifting ground for conscience. This is what I will call "lunar conscience" or the lunar side of conscience. Lunar conscience is based more on the unknown factors of the collective unconscious than on a contemporary society's rules and customs. I conceive of it as representing "mother right" rather than "father right."

Conscience, in both its solar and lunar aspects, is a nonegoistic psychological vertex which demands that the ego sacrifice its own goals and values for a greater, or at least a different, goal or value. But for each of the two types of conscience, the moment of sacrifice is different. Jung writes of this difference as follows:

13

1. I renounce my claim in consideration of a general moral principle, namely that one must not expect repayment for a gift. In this case the "self" coincides with public opinion and the moral code. . . .

2. I renounce my claim because I feel impelled to do so for painful inner reasons which are not altogether clear to me. These reasons give me no particular moral satisfaction; on the contrary, I even feel some resistance to them. But I must yield to the power which suppresses my egoistic claim. (1954, par. 393–394)

In the second case, the demand of conscience is made for murky reasons that are not rationally defended or backed with a reasoned rationale. Its ways appear to be dark and unpredictable, and its laws remain hazy and unidentifiable with general moral imperatives. Personal and individual, it may demand of one person what it does not require of another.

As a lunar phenomenon, conscience is very difficult to predict. What it will demand in the future or in any imagined situation is uncertain, perhaps even fickle. Whereas we can perhaps know, on the basis of even a little self-knowledge, what we will do for the sake of ego or persona, we cannot say with any degree of certainty what we will do "for conscience' sake." Conscience at the lunar level remains free and creative, or at least unpredictable.

Moreover, lunar conscience does not place the highest value on conforming to collective authorities and standards, and in many cases it even turns against the grain of convention and repudiates the collective moral certainties of the day. Coming on as a more or less irrational compulsion, it insists on having its way, dark and insidious as that may appear to be. It is the conscience of the serpent.

Whereas solar conscience demands the sacrifice of egoistic claims for the sake of higher spiritual claims—more noble aims or lofty values—conscience in its lunar aspect poises itself against the ego for apparently lesser claims, perhaps even sinister in nature, antisocial, instinctual, or materialistic. Once we no longer know what God is like in Himself or Herself and are not assured by tradition of the complete revelation of God's ordinances and laws, we are given up to a force whose ways we cannot predict with certainty. In such an ambiguous situation, the ego is also without any sure guide for judging a compulsion and evaluating it: Is it conscience or is it just an indicator of a complex? The ego's knowledge of rules, laws, collective standards, and traditional norms is intact, but it also hears a voice that contradicts them and simply demands, "You must." What the interior advocate asks for is just irrationally the "good," what it denies is the "bad," and the advocating agency behind this intuitive sense lies past the reach of conscious evaluation. Who is speaking? This is a type of conscience whose roots reach deeply into the unconscious.

Solness, the protagonist in Ibsen's *The Master Builder*, states this problem in response to Hilda, who questions him about his motivations. Solness knows that he and Hilda are both driven by trolls, by powers beyond their ego's control. How to evaluate these powers is the question.

> SOLNESS *(eagerly)*. That's it! That's it, Hilda!
> There's a troll in you—same as in me. It's that
> troll in us, don't you see—that's what calls on the
> powers out there. And then we have to give in—
> whether we want to or not.
> HILDA. I almost believe you're right, Mr.
> Solness.

SOLNESS *(walking about the room).* Oh, Hilda,
there are so many devils one can't see loose in the
world!

HILDA. Devils, too?

SOLNESS *(stops).* Good devils and bad devils.
Blond devils and black-haired ones. And if only
you always knew if the light or the dark ones had
you! (Pacing about; with a laugh.) Wouldn't it be
simple then!

(1965, p. 832)

In *Depth Psychology and a New Ethic,* Erich Neumann
observes that "the Voice," as he terms conscience, often demands what might appear to be "evil" from the ego's point of
view, and he recommends that the conflicts which arise from
this should be accepted. Surprisingly often, he says, it is the
avoidance of the conflict which the Voice brings that turns
out to be "unethical" (1969, p. 105).

SOLAR AND LUNAR CONSCIENCE

In this essay, I am using the adjectives *solar* and *lunar* to
denote the poles of a complex psychological unity, conscience.
Conscience in itself I see as an archetype which, like all archetypes, is polar in its structure. Archetypes are basic patterns of human psychological functioning, and while they do
not operate in exactly the same way in each individual, there
are at least hints of them in every human person. I believe
conscience is a universal human experience and perhaps
even extends well into other parts of the animal kingdom in
slightly or greatly altered forms. I have already mentioned
some of the more general characteristics of these two poles
within conscience, and my intention in this essay is to eluci-

date them more thoroughly and to discuss the tensions and relations between them.

The content of views and values on the solar side of conscience is derived from the individual's experience with others, from the many small and large interactions a person has with important others in the family and the wider world, from whom one learns what is customary, appropriate, and politically correct. Solar conscience speaks in and through and for what Jung called the persona. Through this structure, a person incorporates and embodies the values and expectations of parents, teachers, religious figures, and peers. Solar conscience is therefore constituted by culture, and it takes its place within the psychic matrix as the reinforcing backbone of dominant cultural patterns.

When one examines the content of solar conscience, one finds that the values it contains have been carefully laid down and refined through a long collective tradition. Such values can usually be found written down and codified in scriptures and in books of conduct if the culture is literate and in stories and myths if it is oral. Solar conscience can be imaged (and often is so in dreams) as a masculine authority figure or a policeman, whose job is to maintain structures, to preserve the peace, and to thwart aggression, sexuality, and other impulsive or instinctual activities. In a dream, for example, a father or mother will interrupt a bedroom scene. By policing and also by displaying an ideal of the good person, solar conscience contributes to the repression of instinct and impulse and thus assists in the creation of a psychological shadow that is made up of the rejected pieces of the self.

While solar conscience doubtless plays an important role in making possible a person's adaptation to society, and even in making civil society itself possible—for no society could support enough police to watch over every individual (and who would guard the police?)—it is also a strongly negative feature. Often solar conscience takes the form or attitude of a primitive tyrant or even a murderous aggressor against the ego. At this primitive stage of development, solar conscience looks like the mythological child-rejecting Saturn or the child-devouring Kronos (the discussion in chapter two provides more details on these figures). It can have the effect of drying up and withering ego-consciousness with its blistering rays of reproach.

Sandor Rado, a Freudian psychoanalyst, provides a graphic theoretical account of what happens when these abusive internal attacks from solar conscience take place. Rado holds that conscience is built on "retroflected rage," i.e., rage which would naturally be directed outward against an appropriate object such as a father or other authority figure but which, owing to a fear of punishment, is turned back against the ego. Retroflected rage is also, however, derived from a more primitive form of rage that he calls "defiant rage," a rage that would tear down any authority figure who threatens to stop the ego from grabbing full immediate gratification. What happens to form conscience, he contends, is that at some point a bit of this defiant rage deserts its base, forms a psychic institution, and becomes retroflected rage. When the institution of conscience, which was originally built up and fed by the fires of retroflected rage, becomes severe enough, it intensifies the ego's fear of detection to such an extent that one can no longer allow any release of defiant rage: "The enemy, defiant rage, is thus conquered with the aid of its own deserter, retroflected rage" (Rado 1960, p. 328). But now comes the real disaster. Defiant rage becomes channeled into feeding the fires of retroflected rage, and this results in conscience assuming its most catastrophic, blistering, murderous aspect. The image for this is the Terrible Father—Freud's father of the primal herd, who commands death rather than allow his children any access to pleasure.

On the more benevolent side of solar conscience, one can find many images of a Good Father, for instance, the Heavenly Father who would guard and protect his children from harm ("The Lord is my shepherd . . ."), or the life-giving Sun, or the containing and sustaining tradition. Within the solar aspect of conscience there is, therefore, further differentiation. These differentiations I understand to be levels of development from primitive to refined. As the benign voice of the Good Father, solar conscience preserves those orderly forms and institutions of society that shelter and protect us all and without which humanity could not survive.

Lunar conscience, on the other hand, will be conceived as the oracular voice of nature. On this side, conscience insists on what Bachofen classically called "mother right." Mythic images of goddesses like Themis, Dike, and Maat here speak for a sense of order and for a law within the realm of nature itself. Here conscience speaks for an intuition of cosmic order that permeates the natural world and includes humans as conscious creatures within that world. It speaks out of and for "the abysmal side of bodily man," out of and for instinct, body, *materia*. Lunar conscience addresses us not in the patriarchal traditions or through our culturally established moral systems but through the unconscious, in dreams, in complexes, in spontaneous happenings, through instinctual hungers, and also through the inhibitions that lie buried within those hungers.

Like solar conscience, lunar conscience also contains beneficent and punishing facets. It, too, shows levels of development from primitive to refined. On the positive and more refined level, it urges us to nurture ourselves, to allow room and expression for our material and instinctual needs. It is like a good, conscious mother who knows how to keep tabs on her children and anticipate their needs. It tends to the immediacy of things and encourages growth. It urges acceptance and shuns final rejection of any part of the self.

Like the moon, however, lunar conscience has phases, and in its dark phase, the *novilunum*, lies perhaps the most frightening aspect of conscience altogether. Primitive demands for vengeance, psychosomatic tendencies toward disease, and madness as punishment—accompanied by images like the basilisk eye, the rabid bitch, the Furies, the ice-cold queen—are characteristics of this dimension of lunar conscience. Paracelsus describes the condition of a person who is suffering from an attack of lunar conscience as follows:

> Wherever there is a disheartened and timid man in whom imagination has created a great fear and impressed it on him, the moon in heaven aided by her stars is the corpus to bring this about. Whenever such a disheartened man looks at the moon under the full sway of his imagination, he looks into the speculum venenosum magnum naturae (great poisonous mirror of nature), and the sidereal spirit and magnem hominis (mirror of man) will thus be poisoned by the stars and the moon. (Jung 1955–1956, par. 215)

Here is a man looking at the full moon and seeing in it the "great poisonous mirror of nature," the persecutory side of a primitive lunar conscience. It inflicts "a great fear," feelings of becoming unstrung and running at odds with his own nature, threats of lunacy, psychosomatic symptoms, and even disease.

The story of Orestes tells how the dark side of lunar conscience becomes constellated: he murdered his mother! Matricide translates in psychological terms to the severe restriction and repression of nature, instinct, and soma.

CONSCIENCE AS AN EXPONENT
OF WHOLENESS

Conscience has, as I understand it, a bipolar structure, with Sol on the one side and Luna on the other. On each side there is differentiation of levels from primitive to refined. The main goal of conscience is to create an attitude that transcends a narrowly egoistic standpoint, and it does this by proposing ideals and images of harmony and beauty on the one hand and by coercing the disinclined ego by inflicting on it guilt, remorse, conflict, depression, illness, and madness on the other. The paradox of conscience is that it gives voice to both the instinctual and spiritual sides of the self. It is not essentially antihedonic, an "antilibidinal ego" as Guntrip (1989) described.

In the Epistle to the Romans, St. Paul describes, in terms that have become classic for Western culture, the battle between the "law of the flesh" and the "law of the mind." The law of the flesh is most often associated with instinctuality, materialism, the irrational and often dark forces of the unconscious. The biblical tradition has failed to see in the law of the flesh anything but the baser drives of the old Adam. It was in alchemy and other heretical and pagan traditions that the notion of a spirit within nature, an *anima mundi,* was preserved. The law of the mind, on the other hand, is regarded as coming from above, having to do with spirit, logos, the sun. As Jung pointed out, this became the archetype of consciousness for the Christian West, while the mythic figure of Mercurius represents the archetype of the unconscious (Jung 1948, par. 299). Together Mercurius and Christ symbolize the full self, and both have a part within the workings of conscience. But the inevitable conflicts between these two figures produce tensions within conscience itself. Conscience may, at one time, insist on the sacrifice of

21

ego values for a more noble, spiritual value; at another time, it may insist with equal forcefulness on sacrifice for what appears to be simply an instinctual, earthbound value.

As a result of this polarity within conscience, whatever the ego does single-mindedly and one-sidedly "for conscience' sake" may well act to constellate the other tendency, also "for conscience' sake." This paradoxical quality of conscience gives it what Jung called "psychological validity," for at bottom, according to Jung, the essence of the psyche is paradox (Jung 1948, par. 256). Conscience is a true psychological entity. And through the continuous encounter with conscience over a lifetime, a person is forced to encounter and recognize the mystery of what it means to be fully human. In experiencing this genuinely and honestly, we are presented with the opportunity to become what we most truly and essentially are.

Chapter Two

SOLAR CONSCIENCE

Confession is good for the soul, as the saying goes. Jung considered psychotherapy to be an extension in modern guise of the ancient religious practice of confession (cf. Jung 1931, par. 123), and he considered the revealing of deep, dark secrets to be one of the prime threads in any long-term analytic treatment. Sometimes confessing a guilty secret is even sufficient to produce a cure.

Why is this the case? It is because human beings are poorly equipped to carry guilty secrets around in silence. The guilt associated with the secret tortures us, or rather, something within our own personalities tortures us until we spit it out and feel restored. For many, if not most, modern people, punishment for wrongdoing is not reserved for the afterlife. It happens in the present.

William is single, professional, and fortysomething. He has never married, and his secret is sexual. He functions professionally—in the persona—as a community leader and speaks often and with considerable conviction about the importance of high ethical standards and behavior. And yet, he cannot stay away from prostitutes. This is his pain, and it is what he needed to confess in therapy.

One night, he said, he was visiting a family friend and was introduced to a single woman, an artist. They hit it off conversationally and went out for a drink after dinner. She gave no sign of rejecting him sexually, but he did not press her to become intimate on a first date and dropped her off at home in the wee hours. She was a "good girl," he felt, and having put her in that category was uneasy about pursuing a sexual encounter. But since he was sexually stimulated by the conversation, he cruised through a section of the city where he knew streetwalkers hung out. He saw one and stopped, they talked a bit, and she got in his car. As they drove through the darkened streets, she undressed and masturbated him. He dropped her off where he found her, paid her, and wished her good night. He went home sexually relieved but burdened by one more increment added to his guilty secret.

In the therapy session, he was sweating as he confessed this event. His conscience had not let him rest during the intervening days, and he hoped for some relief by telling me about the incident.

By the term *solar conscience,* I am referring to an inner moral guide that represents the values within the thought and behavioral patterns which dominate the conscious life of the individual. Since the dominant conscious patterns of the individual are usually more or less identical to the patterns within contemporary collective life, solar conscience generally speaks for a given society's customs, cultural habits, social laws, and expectations. The images of solar conscience are the typical role models of the culture, usually male ones for men and female ones for women. As the internal advocate of the prevailing moral code, solar conscience speaks largely for the rules and laws which govern the culture and which the populace at large generally accepts as valid restraints on the behavior of the individual.

The underlying principle of solar conscience is that the group takes priority over the individual: the claims of the group outweigh the individual's right to gratify personal wishes and desires. Through the inner agency of solar conscience, the individual's ego is made subject to a group's dominant archetypal patterns. Only within the boundaries laid down by the group's definitions of law and custom should the individual seek private fulfillments and gratifications. Solar conscience demands that we be responsible to society, incorporate the rules and customs of the group's dominant patterns, and take these into consideration even in our most private relationships.

Key to understanding the solar aspect of conscience is realizing that its precepts are generally known and understood. The laws and ideals of the community that are inculcated into the young are inscribed in myths, books, and codes and embodied in the exemplary lives of peers and elders. They are "in the light," observed and recognized by all, and they shine on the individual with the brightness of the sun. Hence the term *solar*.

Once a young person has taken in the socially dominant patterns of behavior, the values which they embody precipitate into the figure of an inner judge who praises or condemns according to the group's customs. The ego is thus exposed to a bright light that can shine into its most secret corners and pass judgment in privacy.

A violation of the norms upheld by solar conscience causes social anxiety in addition to guilt. An ego inwardly accused of infraction by solar conscience experiences the anxiety of banishment and alienation from family, peer group, or tribal community. When duty to the group has gone unfulfilled, or its customs have been violated, or its normative pattern of behavior has been stealthily violated, the ego feels threatened by the fear of isolation and loneliness.

Often this fear leads to remorse, remorse to confession, and confession finally to reinstatement in the group.

A vivid account of this chain of happenings is found in the first chapter of Hermann Hesse's novel *Demian*. As a youth, Demian gets involved with another youngster from "across the tracks," who first tempts him into committing a minor infraction and then threatens to expose him if he does not continue in further collaborations. The threat of blackmail adds to Demian's guilt and anguish, and the resulting misery is exquisitely depicted by Hesse. The fundamental issue is Demian's feeling of alienation from the warmth of family life: suddenly he feels like a person alone, a stranger in his own home. Eventually his pain becomes intolerable, and he confesses his crime to his parents. With great relief, he is restored to the heart of family life.

This circular pattern of crime, followed by guilt and isolation, followed by confession and restoration, is typical within the domain of solar conscience.

Solar conscience, which first extracts the dominant customs and norms of a group and then applies them to the ego, has a further thrust. It elevates such norms into ideals of a highly abstract nature, into ideals like truth, justice, and purity. Through such cognitive abstraction, it can take the most concrete customs of a group and raise them to rarefied levels of perfection, and then it can turn around and apply these abstractions, now as abstract laws and ideals, to the ego. The ego now experiences an ego-ideal of abstract perfection and feels measured against that ideal.

Standards of moral perfection belong to solar conscience. From the vertex of these abstract ideals, the individual can also level judgment against the shortcomings of society at large and against particular individuals and groups within society. They do not measure up. Often this becomes a delightful weapon in the hands of the young to use against parents and the older generation.

THE DEVELOPMENT OF SOLAR CONSCIENCE

Just how the specific contents of solar conscience become vested in the individual is a complex question, and many psychologists, notably Freud and Piaget, have puzzled about it. Observation of infant behavior indicates the absence of an inborn sense of right and wrong as these terms are defined by a family and a culture. The infant does not inherit knowledge of a moral nature, nor are the archetypal patterns which dominate the parents' and culture's attitudes strongly and visibly present and constellated in the individual at birth.

Yet already in the first months and certainly by the age of one year it is possible to see a child's disposition toward obedience and disobedience to the parents' wishes and directions. While the child may not understand the specific meaning of a parent's words, he or she does sense the general nature of a directive and responds accordingly. This may show itself as a slight pause when the child hears a scolding tone or a threat in a parent's voice.

Robert Scholl, in his book *The Conscience of the Child,* argues quite persuasively that the roots of this aspect of conscience lie in a child's relationship to parents, and particularly in the relationship to the mother. Scholl says the child experiences a pleasurable sense of harmony with the mother until some sort of misbehavior occurs. Then the relationship becomes disturbed, and this creates anxiety in the infant. The child tries to restore the original harmony through reparation and good behavior. This would be behavior that pleases the mother and elicits warmth and tenderness from her, a smile. As memory increases, the child learns what pleases and what displeases the parent and seeks to please, finally, even in situations where discovery is unlikely. The entire drama now can play itself out internally. "This," writes

Scholl, "is the moment when conscience is born" (1970, p. 27). In the language I am using, this is the moment when the solar aspect of conscience congeals sufficiently in the psyche so that the particular contents presented by family and culture can take up firm residence within it and be applied to the ego. Until this point, solar conscience has been structurally latent in the psyche, un-constellated and unconscious.

According to Scholl, the precondition for conscience is the infant's fundamental feeling of security in a harmonious relationship with the mother, in the feeling of being embedded in and protected by her. The deeper this feeling, the more profoundly will a child be disturbed by the contrary feelings of disruption and disharmony and the stronger therefore will be the child's conscience (Scholl 1970, p. 29). At this pre-oedipal level of solar conscience, the ego's reward for good behavior is harmony with the mother, and the punishment for unacceptable behavior is the anxiety brought about by falling out of harmony with her, a frightening sense of vulnerability and isolation. The solar side of conscience is attuned to the world outside, and the first person it tunes in to is the mother.

Solar conscience becomes constellated—is born out of the waters of the unconscious, so to speak—as the ego develops its capacities for memory and attunement with the environment. Not yet itself a fully autonomous and separate psychic entity, the ego in these early phases relies heavily on projective identification with persons in the environment, primarily the mother. As the infant's ego develops coherence out of the matrix of an undifferentiated self, the solar aspect of the conscience archetype becomes projected upon the primary parent in the child's environment. The anxiety that the child experiences when harmony with the parent is threatened is, therefore, exceedingly deep, for the ego–self axis has little reliability or stability at this point. The threat of its collapse provokes terrifying abandonment anxiety within the fledgling ego complex.

The ego, which precipitates gradually out from oceanic union with the preexistent Self, depends radically for its unity and stability upon the carriers of projective identification, the parents. These persons are the objects in terms of which the infant person will define herself, and they make it possible for her to become born in the psychological sense of having a separate ego. Thus born into the context of a specific parental and family environment, the norms of attitude and behavior then enter the child by osmosis.

The stability of the ego's sense of integrity and well-being comes to depend on having positive relations to these parentally sponsored customs and norms and on the observance of them. The child's earliest perceptions of right and wrong are mediated through this relation to the family milieu, and they are concrete in nature. What the parents concretely approve and disapprove of becomes a kind of protolegal structure. If the parents mediate the standard conventions and collective norms of society, the child will learn, through molding to the parents, the basic adaptational mores specific to the culture. If, on the other hand, the parents mediate values and attitudes which do not correspond to the typical dominant patterns of society at large, the child's later adaptation to society will be conflicted and problematic.

As children leave their primary dependence on the mother, the father takes over as the principal carrier of the projection of conscience, and this development marks a deep divide within conscience. One pole of it becomes identified with the father, while the other pole remains behind with the mother. The portion of conscience that becomes attached to the father image develops into what I am calling solar conscience. The portion that remains with the mother will develop into what I will call lunar conscience (in the next chapter). This moment when the transference changes and the father enters the picture as an available projection carrier bifurcates conscience and leaves it forever after changed. It becomes a two-story structure, so to speak.

In patriarchal society, especially, the father represents to the family the dominant social patterns and values regnant in the wider cultural world. The father mediates the cultural world to the children and introduces them to the nonpersonal world of social expectations outside of the home and outside of the domain of intimate interpersonal relations.

Thus, while the foundations of conscience lie in the child's relations to the mother, the solar structures of it are much more heavily determined by the father and his psychological heirs.

The father's influence in introducing social values and ideals into the organization of solar conscience is later reduced or displaced by the peer group. If a father is not present in the family, this transference to a peer group may take place much earlier than if a strong father figure exists in the family. Now the contents of solar conscience become located in the peer group through the dynamic of projective identification, and the ego seeks to maintain its identity and stability through conformity with peer values. The value- and ideal-determining function of the peer group is particularly strong during adolescence, when mother and father are generally debased as ideals and carriers of idealized projections. Solar conscience now adopts values and ideals that are more in harmony with the attitudes of peers and are held up by them as shining truths. The anxiety created by violating solar conscience at this point has the quality of social ostracism and isolation. This gives the adolescent gang enormous power and authority over the individual.

In still later development, during early adult and adult years, the projection of solar conscience tends to pass over to professional groups, to the accepted collective religion of the tribe or family, or to society's more general customs, laws, and norms. Professional group, religion, and culture now feed contents directly into solar conscience, and the ego seeks to adjust itself to the more adult values of living a responsible life within society at large and to establish a harmonious relationship to collective consciousness.

Often at some point in psychological and cognitive development, solar conscience lifts off from concrete rules and customs and becomes more abstract and transcendent. Reflection transforms the concrete expectations and moral persuasions of the immediate culture or group into impersonal and abstract values. These now become philosophical or even theological. Perhaps as a part of the detachment that takes place within the parent–child relationship, solar conscience moves out, up, and away from the here-and-now into the realm of universal spiritual principles and laws. There seems to be an inherent affinity for logos within solar conscience. While it passes through projective identification with quite specific figures, such as mother, father, peer group leader, and teacher, it does not rest content with the concrete carriers who represent an ego-ideal. It seeks, instead, to ascend toward the principles and abstract laws which these persons or collectives may represent for a time. In this movement toward abstraction, the individual distills the spiritual values and ideals from the concrete moral and spiritual atmosphere surrounding the carriers of solar conscience imperatives. The ego may experience this movement as a kind of moral enlightenment, experiencing such ideals as truth, justice, and mercy as numinous in and of themselves. These values now no longer need to be represented by anyone in particular. They can subsist in themselves.

This was the experiential background of the great biblical prophets, out of which they penned such immortal and stirring lines as "let justice roll down like waters, and righteousness like an ever-flowing stream" (Amos 5:24), appealing to others who shared a similar inner experience of "justice" and "righteousness," in and of themselves high abstractions. As Kant states in his account of the ethical imperative, there is an intuition of eternal law inscribed in the soul. The entry into solar conscience of this Apollonic energy for transcendence and clarity of principles is by no means inevitable, but the tendency or potential for it seems to belong to the dynamic of the solar aspect of conscience.

Moving away from specific moral habits toward the principles and spiritual ideals underlying dominant cultural patterns, solar conscience leads the ego away from attachment to concrete figures into a kind of love affair with law and principle themselves, into a deep and passionate commitment to the abstract values underlying a specific cultural or religious tradition. The Bible expresses this exquisitely:

> With my whole heart have I sought thee:
> O let me not wander from thy commandments!
> (Psalms 119:10)

> I will meditate in thy precepts,
>   and have respect unto thy ways.
> I will delight myself in thy statutes;
>   I will not forget thy word.
> (Psalms 119:15–16)

Oh, how love I thy law!
   it is my meditation all the day.
(Psalms 119:97)

From solar conscience, then, the voice of God speaks in laws and precepts. These laws can be learned, are often written down in holy books, and form the abstract spiritual foundations of specific cultural and religious traditions. This body of law invariably is seen to originate *in illo tempore,* in a mythic time long ago when God, at a special moment, chose to reveal the divine commandments (Eliade 1963). Through the workings of solar conscience, the spiritual heritage of law and precept become housed in the individual and elevated to the transcendental level of *vox Dei* (the "voice of God"). Thus solar conscience can recapitulate, in a way, the moment of original revelation when it speaks from within of law and precept.

The question of the intensity and quality of solar conscience in an individual must be related to developmental failures and impasses. If solar conscience is never constellated as a psychic factor in the life of a given individual, it means the relationship with the mother was highly disturbed and perhaps nonexistent, emotionally or physically. The absence of conscience indicates autism, that is, a profound lack of relationship, in at least one important sector of psychic existence. There never was an attachment between mother and infant, hence there was also no opportunity for projective identification with her and no abandonment anxiety. The originating energy of conscience is absent, and solar conscience is therefore never established. It remains deeply unconscious and structurally unconstellated in the sense of forming a determinative relationship over against the ego. This kind of person has a completely unconscious, or latent, solar conscience.

This may not mean that solar conscience is completely inactive even so, however. It may carry out its work quite effectively but unconsciously. A sociopathic criminal will unintentionally leave traces of identity behind at the scene of the crime in order to allow detection. Such slips provide evidence for the view that there is a conscience at work unbeknownst to the ego, a conscience which may not be able to produce guilt and anxiety in the ego but can produce punishment nevertheless from external sources. This sociopathic personality will act out conscience by producing scenes in which guilt and punishment are experienced from external agencies like police and courts. A spouse who inadvertently leaves evidence of an affair for the partner to discover is doing the same thing. But these phenomena belong more readily in the discussion of lunar conscience, which I will take up in the following chapter.

Solar conscience may not take the turn toward abstraction described above but rather remain fixed at concrete levels. This depends on cognitive development in other areas. If there is an arrest at this level of cognitive functioning generally, then solar conscience cannot rise above it. Or it is also possible that cognitive development takes place intellectually but not within solar conscience because of a fixation of projective identification upon a concrete carrier of it and the ego's inability to separate from this beloved object. The Apollonic tendency toward abstraction that we see to be such an inherent part of solar conscience is, in such a case, blocked by a stronger need to remain contained in an emotional relationship. Abstraction threatens this relationship, and separation anxiety is greater than the need for development.

THE RELATIONS BETWEEN
SOLAR CONSCIENCE AND EGO

While the earliest period in the constellation of solar conscience is clearly to be located within the mother–infant relationship, the definitive shape and feeling quality of the matured solar entity has more to do with the subsequent relationship between father and child. As already stated, this is the case because the father introduces the cultural world into the psychological life of a person in a way that the mother generally does not, at least in the earliest phases of development. Mother provides the experience of mutuality and intimacy, and she creates a personal world of attachment and emotional bonds. Father presents to the child the impersonal world of social custom and norm, a world of cultural expectations for attitude and behavior. Solar conscience moves toward abstraction, hence it passes from mother to father and later to peer group, to society at large, and finally to law and rule in and of themselves.

The relation between the ego and solar conscience is therefore importantly affected by the relationship between a person and his or her father. Freud's anthropological speculation about a primal horde with a brutal, overbearing father and his at first subservient, then rebellious, sons as the phylogenetic ancestor of the relation between superego and ego is one statement of how this relation may be conceived. But it is not the only one, and in what follows I hope to add other features to this picture.

In images of the father–child relationship as depicted in myth, religion, and fairy tale, we can find various possibilities for how the ego–solar conscience relation may look. Solar conscience can relate to the ego in all the ways a father can relate to his child. Considering all these possibilities and nuances, there are two extreme positions: 1) father and child may enjoy a relationship characterized by respect and an attitude of benevolence; or 2) father and child may have a relationship tortured by tyranny, victimization, and rebellion. For individuals, matters generally lie somewhere between these extremes and perhaps tend to fluctuate a good bit according to situation, mood, intensity of drive, etc.

In his beneficent aspect, a father rewards a person for good behavior with feelings of accomplishment, competence, inclusion, and self-satisfaction. His demands and ideals are not impossibly high and unattainable, and the price he exacts by way of sacrifice of ego wishes and desires is not too exorbitant. He even protects the ego from becoming overly scrupulous and perfectionistic. He is benevolent.

In his negative aspect, the father is seen as a devourer who swallows his children, who represses them and constricts their harmless spontaneities. He punishes them with crippling remorse and guilt and threatens them with isolation and exile from the human community.

When Freud first put forward his theory of the superego, he found little good in it. It was seen as driven by harsh self-aggression and by the death wish. This attitude toward conscience and culture may have its reasons in modern history. Jung observes:

> This higher world [i.e., of the Spirit] has an impersonal character and consists on the one hand of all those traditional, intellectual, and moral values which educate and cultivate the individual, and, on the other hand, of the products of the unconscious, which present themselves to consciousness as archetypal ideas. Usually the former predominate. But when, weakened by age or criticism, they lose their power of conviction, the archetypal ideas rush in to fill the gap. Freud, correctly recognizing this situation, called the traditional values "superego," but the archetypal ideas remained unknown to him. (1955–1956, par. 673)

The traditional values by themselves, when imposed upon an individual's ego without meaning or rationality through the medium of a tired and worn-out civilization, can be experienced as a senseless tyranny better overthrown and eliminated. This was clearly the cultural climate in Hapsburg Vienna at the turn of the century. In this historical milieu, Freud's image of a brutal father in a primal horde as the basis of superego has its sense. Would this not resemble the Hapsburg Emperor?

For a contrast to this view of solar conscience, however, one can look to sayings of Jesus about the Father, to oriental ancestor worship, and to the many stories, myths, and fairy tales in which fathers are positively and helpfully related to their children.

For the psychotherapist, however, the negative images of the father as depictions of solar conscience are more fascinating. They are the ones who represent the problematic nature of solar conscience, and these images are familiar to anyone who works in depth with people's souls. To consider a portion of the range of possibilities for this negative relation between solar conscience and the ego, I will focus on three well-known father images from Greek mythology: Uranus, Kronos, and Zeus. These three figures represent a development within three generations of fathers, and one cannot help but speculate that this represents a development of solar conscience within Greek culture.

As mythical fathers, Uranus and Kronos are largely identical. Both severely suppress their children, the first by shoving them back into their mother Gaia, the second by swallowing them whole and holding them captive in his stomach. But as images of solar conscience, there are subtle and important differences to note.

URANUS

Uranus, the most ancient and primal of the Greek Great Father deities, is depicted by Hesiod to be the son of Gaia, the Earth, who was the First Principle. As Father Sky, Uranus was thought to descend each night and cover Gaia, and from their incestuous cohabitation there sprang a number of children, called the Titans. Male and female alike, these children were not tolerated by Uranus, and he pressed them back into the womb, back into Mother Earth, where they stagnated for lack of activity and freedom. Eventually one of them, Kronos, was secretly removed from the womb by Mother Gaia, and when Father Uranus descended that night, this rebellious and angry Titanic son castrated him. He then released his brothers and sisters, and so began the age of the Titans.

The father–child relationship in the Uranus constellation is characterized by vast distance: Uranus is sky, and his children are locked deep within the womb of earth. In Jane Harrison's view, there is an important distinction between *ta metarsia* (the highest heavens, the ether) and *ta meteopa* (the lower heavens, weather). Uranus governs both but belongs more to the former. Uranus, she says, represents "the whole might of the upper air," and out of him several "Titans specialize into Sun-Gods" (1912, pp. 454–455).

Plato, in the dialogue *Cratylus,* states that Uranus is "rightly so called from looking upward," and he goes on to indicate that looking upward is the way to gain a pure mind (Hamilton and Cairns 1961, p. 434). In *Epinomis,* he names Uranus the highest of the gods and puts him in charge of teaching wisdom through mathematics and of exerting distant control over the stars and seasons in their regular motions, thereby ensuring that even the "very slowest creature

. . . on which God has bestowed the capacity to learn" will pick up at least the basic skills of counting (ibid., pp. 1520–1521).

In astrology, according to Sigrid Strauss-Kloebe, Uranus has to do with "transcendence, spacelessness, and timelessness." Uranus, she goes on,

> knows nothing of causality and continuity. According to the horoscope, Uranus is presented as a creative power that suddenly breaks forth out of an incomprehensible background; as a power that was previously unknown, is new, whether for good or ill, seemingly unconnected to the world of appearances; who seems able to appear only as this kind of creative invasion and has no interest in permanence or steady achievement, but fulfills himself in the moment. (1934, p. 443)

For the children of Uranus, locked away as they are in the concreteness of Earth, the father must seem entirely absent and incomprehensible. He is also an enemy. What he represents is unknown to them. The high spirituality of Uranus is unavailable, and their relationship to him is conflicted and enigmatic.

That they have no access to him and to his spirit does not mean that they do not suffer from his repressing force. On the contrary, it is precisely he who keeps them in the dark. They are trapped in the mother, but indirectly under the thumb of the father who will not allow them more separation and autonomy.

In the Uranus constellation, the ego remains primarily a mother's child. Of this kind of psychological situation, Erich Neumann, in his massive and masterful study of the Great Mother archetype, writes: "with mothers' sons the father-god is eclipsed by the Terrible Mother, and they themselves are unconsciously held fast in the womb and cut off from the creative, solar side" (1974, p. 189). Removed from the spiritual potential offered by a relationship with the father, they nevertheless suffer his repressive influence. Because they remain trapped and contained within the mother, solar conscience in these psyches cannot rise beyond the concrete and dogmatic level of abstraction. Lacking access to the spirit of the law, the ego fixes upon the letter, upon specific concrete customs and rules of the group, and remains dependent and attached to specific figures of authority in the environment whom it is always essential to please. Particular customs, laws, and traditions, just because they belong intrinsically to the matrix of culture, come to carry the force of absolute verities. This becomes a fundamentalism of solar conscience.

If solar conscience becomes fixated at the Uranus grade, we see a kind of blind traditionalism and primitive, unreflective conservatism. The contents of solar conscience consist here of moral habits and reactions that are adhered to unconsciously, performed automatically and more or less without conscious conflict. These contents are social and cultural expectations that one endures without questioning why, only knowing that it would be an egregious breach of decorum to do otherwise. These cultural habits and patterns are imposed by the active, if unrecognized, agency of solar conscience, and to ignore them or refuse them brings on anxiety, guilt, and fear of isolation. Here, a person lives at the level of a culture's matrix, which states the unconscious or only half-conscious assumptions, customs, expectations, and habits that distinguish an Englishman from an Italian or a Frenchman from a Texan.

If the Uranus grade dominates and characterizes solar conscience in an individual, we find some further characteristic movements within the psyche. The symbols of Uranus are the lightning axe and the bird (Harrison 1912, p. 176), and these aptly characterize the way in which he "strikes." Uranian solar conscience strikes as a spontaneous fear or a sudden anxious thought that flashes danger. It feels like an anxiety attack. Children of Uranus are bound within the mother and are unusually subject to blind repetitiveness of rote behavior. They live also under the threat of a father whose rigidity and suspicion are signs of his insecurity. Such a person tends to be docile, compliant, and extremely fearful of abusive authority figures. There is little capacity here for moral reflection or innovation, only for consulting rule books and etiquette guides.

KRONOS

Following Hesiod, movement out of this Uranus constellation begins when Gaia becomes disgruntled with the burden of the children who have been stuffed back into her. Gaia's discomfort, due to the heaviness and pressure of these Titanic children in her womb, heralds the beginning of a plan in which she plots to overthrow her husband-son, Uranus, through a heroic child, Kronos.

In an individual, this situation is spelled out psychologically in the picture of placid obedience to the canons of collective morality within consciousness while dreaming and fantasizing about rebellion. Frustration, conflict, and anger quietly build up inside and gather around a still deeply unconscious but potentially heroic determination to change.

The explosive elevation of Kronos has a revolutionary transformative effect upon ego-consciousness. There is a dramatic reversal of attitude within consciousness. The formerly placid child becomes a rebellious teenager, the docile and overweight housewife a tiger. In classical times, this type of reversal of role and attitude was enacted in the ancient Kronian and Saturnalian festivals of Greece and Rome.

41

The festival of Kronos (Saturn) was celebrated during the vernal equinox, when the sun breaks out of winter into spring (cf. Harrison 1912, p. 252). On this day, "it is the custom," wrote Athenaeus,

> to feast the slaves, the masters themselves undertaking for the nonce the office of servants. The custom is also Greek. . . . a similar practice prevails in Crete at the Hermaea: the slaves are feasted and make merry, while their masters perform the menial offices. (In Harrison 1912, p. 251)

Among the Boeotians, according to Plutarch, this day "was called the day of the Good Spirit," and the spirits of the dead were released for the day "from the prison of the grave" (ibid., p. 253). On this day, too, the old king is driven out and replaced by a new and vigorous young spirit (ibid., p. 223). Thus, the uprising of Kronos is characterized by radical social and psychological turmoil, by the inversion of values, by enjoyment of freedom and open possibility, and a violent, revolutionary attitude toward the old, dying order.

Despite all this turbulence and revolutionary zeal, however, things do not essentially change. It is but a momentary revolution, perhaps even a "king for a day" charade, for the next day the slaves are once again in their quarters and the masters in their palaces. For Kronos is not much different from his father Uranus, mostly only another version of the same anxieties.

Kronos, too, suppresses his children. After he mates with his sister Rhea and their union becomes fruitful, Rhea gives birth to a number of children of both genders. Kronos then proceeds to become uneasy, as his father was in the generation before him, because of an oracle predicting that one of his children will overthrow him as he overthrew his father. So Kronos swallows his children whole. He is the type of father who devours his children's lives by coopting their psychological and spiritual independence. He takes them up into himself. So what appears to be a revolutionary change in solar conscience is not really so great after all. There is change within solar conscience, to be sure, and it is characterized by cognitive development and the release of potential for spiritualizing values and ideals. Meanings and principles are extracted from the concrete customs and mores, and there is a development of the notion of law. But the relation of solar conscience to the ego remains harsh, repressive, and now also devouring.

Through this development from Uranian to Kronian structure, solar conscience becomes more omnipresent and steady in its influence. Before it was momentary and arbitrary, striking like a paroxysm of anxiety, a panic attack. Now solar ideals and spiritual values come to stand over the ego in the image of a constant taskmaster, a sun that burns hot and bright over the noonday fields below, a father in heaven who watches and records thoughts and deeds. That heavy and continuous sense of duty, which is generally lauded by moral philosophers as the most desirable and praiseworthy ethical stance, comes into play. Duty is now defined, however, not as obedience to concrete figures in the environment or to specific cultural requirements, but to the spirit or the idea of relationships or of culture, to ideals such as truth and justice, mercy and righteousness. As a result, a person experiences, according to Erich Neumann, the loss of "consciousness of his dual nature through separation from his earthly parts, his instincts" (Neumann 1954, p. 187). Kronos takes his children into himself, radically separating them from the earth, their bodies and their instincts, and there he holds them in thrall to abstract spiritual ideals and values. This is biblical man.

At the Kronos level of structure, solar conscience judges according to the highest and most exacting principles and ideals, seeing sharply through sham and charade and moral compromise, and it is capable of inflicting inwardly feelings of shame and guilt over fantasies and acts that depart from ideals of purity and moral perfection.

These are people with a highly sensitive conscience. Ibsen's master builder, Solness, is such a character. He blames himself for the fire that destroyed the house his wife brought into the marriage, an event which allowed him to become a great success but also wrecked his marriage and family. After he explains his tortured reasoning to the young woman, Hilda, they have the following exchange:

> HILDA *(looking at him attentively)*. You are ill, Mr. Solness. Very ill, I almost think.
>
> SOLNESS. Insane. You can say it. It's what you mean.
>
> HILDA. No, I don't think you've lost your reason.
>
> SOLNESS. What, then? Out with it!
>
> HILDA. I'm wondering if maybe you didn't enter life with a frail conscience.
>
> SOLNESS. A frail conscience? What in hell's name does that mean?
>
> HILDA. I mean your conscience is very fragile. Over-refined, sort of. It isn't made to struggle with things—to pick up what's heavy and bear it.
>
> SOLNESS *(growling)*. Hm! And what kind of conscience do you recommend?
>
> HILDA. I could wish that your conscience was—well, quite robust.

SOLNESS. Oh? Robust? And I suppose you have
a robust conscience?

HILDA. Yes, I think so. I've never noticed it
wasn't.

SOLNESS. I'd say you've never had a real test to
face up to, either.

(Ibsen 1965, p. 831)

What Ibsen has done in this masterful play is to translate
the intuitions of Greek tragedy, which always takes place
through fated events and historical enactment, onto the
stage of inner experience, of interiority. As Jung said, the
gods have not disappeared, they have become our diseases
(1957, par. 54). What the Greeks projected as Kronos and
the Latins as Saturn, we moderns experience as conscience.
And a child of Kronos-Saturn looks a lot like Solness, the
master builder with a chronic sense of guilt and a remorse-
lessly burning conscience.

The mythic Kronos himself lives under threat of insur-
rection and violent overthrow. The fear of upheaval and dethronement undergirds his rigidity, and a subtle and pervasive suspiciousness, often found in the subtle background of
father–child relationships as well as written into the legal
statutes of societies, distinguishes his rule. An example of
extreme Kronian defensiveness can be found encoded in a
document entitled "Acts and Laws of the Colony of Connecti-
cut," promulgated in 1715, listing twelve capital crimes,
among them the following:

> If any Man have a Stubborn and Rebellious Son of suf-
> ficient understanding, viz., sixteen years of age, which
> will not Obey the Voice of his Father or the Voice of his
> Mother, and that when they have Chastised him he
> will not Hearken unto them, then may his Father or
> Mother, being his Natural Parents, lay hold on him,

and bring him to the Magistrates Assembled in Court,
and Testify unto them that their Son is Stubborn and
Rebellious . . . and such a Son shall be Put to Death.
(quoted by Alsop 1972)

It is this kind of cruel, authoritarian attitude that Kronos
conscience can inject into cultural and family values and use
to govern the ego.

But this fails to tell the whole story of Kronos and the
influence of this type of solar conscience on the psyche. There
is another side to Kronos, a more benign and positive aspect.
In this, the positive side of solar conscience can be seen.
Plato, the Heracliteans, and the Orphics identified Kronos
with *eniautos,* "he who has all things in himself" (Harrison
1912, p. 186). In the festivals of the new year, Kronos was
presented as *eniautos-daimon,* a fertility spirit (ibid., p. 223).
To understand the fertility of Kronos and of solar conscience,
one must look at the potential value of the conflicts that this
type of solar conscience creates within ego-consciousness.

Kronos frees a person from the mother, from concrete
identification with the body and unity with instincts, and
puts up a barrier against automatic and unreflective gratification of impulses. On the one hand, Kronian solar conscience attracts with lofty ideals; on the other, it punishes
with guilt. One important result of such an *opus contra
naturam* is, Jung points out, greater awareness:

> Man in his "natural" condition is neither good nor pure,
> and if he should develop in the natural way the result
> would be a product not essentially different from an
> animal. Sheer instinctuality and naive unconscious-
> ness untroubled by a sense of guilt would prevail if the
> Master had not interrupted the free development of
> the natural being by introducing a distinction between
> good and evil and outlawing the evil. Since without
> guilt there is no moral consciousness and without

awareness of differences no consciousness at all, we must concede that the strange intervention of the master of souls was absolutely necessary for the development of any kind of consciousness and in this sense was for the good. (1948, par. 244)

Solar conscience plays a part in the ongoing, distinction-making, differentiating function of consciousness, adding the moral element as a continuous player in it. The specific contribution of Kronos in this process of consciousness-making is to introduce a kind of glue or cement to keep moral consciousness from being washed away by complexes, emotions, impulses, and drives. Solar conscience tightens the pitch of the distinction between good and evil, and it brings their polarized relationship into a more rigorous tension. It is in the creation of this tension that we find the meaning of Kronos-Saturn's designation as a fertility spirit.

It is the nature of Kronos-Saturn to set sharp boundaries and define borders. He also constricts. The metal of Saturn was considered to be lead. James Hillman writes that "certain kinds of sexual disorder could be controlled by means of lead, according to Albertus Magnus: 'The effect of lead is cold and constricting, and it has a special power over sexual lust and nocturnal emissions'" (1970, p. 155).

Kronos-Saturn constricts the flow of libidinous desire; he is the god of sexual impotence. But constriction and impotence do not necessarily constitute a blind alley. As Hillman writes, "sexuality would exhaust itself in exteriority, the copulative delights, the ceaseless generation," while Kronos can lead to a "heightened power of imagination" (ibid.).

While Kronos sets boundaries, constricts, and tightens the tension between the opposites good and evil, he also concentrates, coagulates, and lends the attitudes of ego-consciousness firmness and weight. The concentration of attention on moral imagination, blocking as it does extraverted expansiveness, leads to the extraordinary power of the small—the power of the pen, of symbolic representations, of art. Diodorus claimed that Kronos introduced the civilized manner of life to human culture (Harrison 1912, p. 252). The power of the small and of moral imagination are aspects of what we usually call character. Such a development of personality is certainly in the interest of culture and of the social order, but it may also serve the interest of furthering the individual's personal development. Without a streak of chronic morality, one would not be bothered by coming upon the shadow, and one would not respond with "the violent aversion everybody feels when he has to see through his projections and recognize the nature of the anima" (Jung 1955–1956, par. 674). The result of an attitude of pure untrammeled naturalism would be "that the insight is robbed of its efficacy, since the moral reaction is missing" (ibid.). Indeed, one would be seduced all too easily into living out the impulses of the shadow and the fantasies of the anima. If this tendency prevailed, the process of individuation would come to little result (in alchemical imagery, Mercurius would escape the vessel), for the shadow and the anima will not yield up their treasures without having to confront resistance from the ego. The enforcer of this moral resistance—sometimes brutal, uncompromising, and always deaf to seduction—is Kronian solar conscience.

An analysand once presented the following dream:

> I am in a pool of water; the pool is surrounded by a garden, with trees, flowers, and shrubs, and running around the entire garden is a fence. I look up toward the gate and see an animal, a snake-alligator, standing upright on its hind legs, testing the gate and trying to get out. Afraid that he will indeed manage to get out, I stand and watch. Finally he gets through the gate and disappears. Now I am running down the side

of a hill, lightly, as though I could fly. Toward the bottom I suddenly come upon several open graves; in one of them is lying the snake-alligator, dead, appearing to be stuffed . . .

The dreamer was a young man with serious problems in his marriage. Shortly before the dream, he had an extramarital affair. He thought that the dream pointed to castration anxiety (the death of the snake-alligator, which he saw as a symbol for the penis), and that this castrating force came from without, since he felt no guilt about the affair.

The pool and garden are familiar images in dream and art, and they point in this instance to the transference and the analytical situation. The figure of the analyst is absent, so whatever controlling force he might exert is missing, and the containment of the snake-alligator is left to the fence and the gate. The fence, the gate, the boundary, on and off limits—such images indicate the activity and role of Kronian solar conscience. Here these boundaries pertain to the analytical work, and they form the container for what might be released in this work. We see here the alchemical problem of keeping the stopper in the vessel and containing the spirit Mercurius.

What is released from the unconscious in this dream is represented by the snake-alligator. There are many possible meanings and amplifications for the snake and alligator. Some of those pertinent to this case are the following. The snake symbolizes perhaps the most numinous, threatening, fascinating, and unconscious depths of the psyche; it poisons and can heal; it contains the opposites of matter and spirit and often symbolizes the spirit of the unconscious itself. In this case, it is both phallic and spiritual (indicated by the turgid, upright, quasi-human position). The snake symbol includes, further, the attributes of the alligator, a usually threatening, sharp-toothed, maternal monster.

This animal, which analysis has released from the pool of the unconscious, wants to move outward beyond the boundaries of analysis into the outside world. This direction outward, into concrete realization of fantasy, was characteristic of this analysand's conscious attitude: unless a fantasy could be acted out, it was considered worthless. But the dream ego knows the danger of acting out, and because of this fear it has a secret sort of alliance with the fence and the gate. When the snake-alligator escapes, extensity is paid for with loss of intensity. The animal spends itself, and out there it dies or is killed.

That the gate cannot hold the impulse indicates a structural weakness in the retaining barriers of Kronian solar conscience. In cases like this one, where a containing psychological attitude is absent and one sees a lack of capacity to hold a powerful surge of libido within consciousness long enough to analyze it and work it through, a task of the analyst is to reinforce and strengthen the gate, the Kronian solar conscience. The psychologically minded analyst would do this not primarily in the interests of society (although that may also be a strong motive), but for the sake of the analysand's own personal growth. When the snake-alligator is held, or faced, and fought, the personality gains a creative vigor and a depth of intensity otherwise missing, and this promises to lead to underground sources of wealth and energy otherwise unavailable. This holding back of animal nature depends on the strength and integrity of the fence and the gate.

The intense creative power of the small is the child of Kronos *eniautos,* "he who holds all things in himself."

When Kronian solar conscience—with its lofty spiritual ideals, its highly critical attitude that burns steadily downward like the noonday sun, and its rigid ethical demands— is turned toward the ego, it governs through the ego-ideal and the threat of ferocious guilt. It can also turn its attention to society and, through visions of utopia, impose a strenuous critique upon the usually casual workings and compromised political settlements of collective life. Social utopians, from Plato and the biblical prophets through Thomas More, Marx, and Engels, down to present-day radicals, stand under the influence and tutelage of a Kronian solar conscience whose gaze looks outward. In Kronos, we find a kind of solar social conscience that is not satisfied with occasional works of charity. The social utopian wants to reorganize the basic structures of society according to a system of abstract ideals and norms and standards.

Plato describes the "age of Kronos" with images of paradise that characterize, more or less, all visions of utopia:

> ... the god, in his kindness to man ... set over us this superior race of spirits who took charge of us with no less ease to themselves than a convenience to us, providing us with peace and mercy, sound law and unscanted justice, and endowing the families of mankind with internal concord and happiness. (Hamilton and Cairns 1961, pp. 1304–1305)

In this imagined utopian society, savagery was absent and there was no preying of creature on creature, no war or any strife whatsoever. When the god Kronos was shepherd, there were no political constitutions, no taking of wives, no begetting of children. New persons came directly out of the earth and had no memory of former things. There were no grudges. There were fruits and vegetables without stint from trees and plants, and these needed no cultivation but sprang up of themselves out of the ground without human effort. Humans went about in the open needing neither clothing nor shelter, for the seasons were blended so evenly that there was no hurt to anyone, and the grass that sprang up out of the earth in abundance made a soft bed for them (ibid., p. 1037).

In the golden age of Kronos, as Plato depicts it, humans did not rule over others, just as we do not put goats in charge of goats or oxen of oxen, but the god divided the world into regions of kingdoms and placed superior spirits over each part. Here we see again the notion of the superiority of the ideal: spirits cannot be corrupted or bribed, and political compromises and accommodations are therefore out of the question.

As visionary social awareness, Kronian solar conscience "sees to bone," "cuts through the crap," launches a radical critique, and creates ideal basic structures with utopian dimensions. In this, of course, lies a livid streak of root-and-branch destructiveness, a violent impulse to emasculate the old order, to tear down and burn, and to regard all ideological doubters as the enemy, whose only just reward is consignment to the sulfurous pit:

> . . . the godless and unrighteous man departs to the prison of vengeance and punishment which they call Tartaros. (Plato, *Gorgias,* in Hamilton and Cairns 1961, p. 304)

Measuring friend and enemy against ideological standards and ideal norms, regarding all those who are not for us as against us, punishing offenders with banishment, torture, and disgrace—all of this inflexible "justice," unmitigated by mercy and understanding of human weakness, belongs to the Kronian field. This imagery and vivid notion of post-mortal punishment for sin is also deeply ingrained in the Christian tradition. In modern persons, this is internalized and experienced in ways depicted by figures like Solness in Ibsen's *The Master Builder*.

The effect of radical critiques and utopian visions on society is shock, tension, defensiveness, and self-consciousness on the part of rulers. And in so tightening the pitch and increasing the tension lies the creative potential of the action of Kronian solar conscience. The cynical flexibility of politicians is challenged, the locked doors of power brokers are burst open, and the most sacrosanct assumptions of aristocratic irresponsibility are called into question. The Kronian social critics sniff out the dung, the rot, the corruption in the shadows of the power merchants and expose their findings to the light of collective consciousness. They are today's investigative journalists. And this spreading out of the manure of moral corruption and exposing it to the light of ethical reflection fertilizes collective life by driving society out of lethargy and stagnation into movement, pressing it inch by inch toward images of a more ideal social order. Even if the radical Kronian critics manage to produce only reactionary hardening among the power elite, they still serve to raise the level of consciousness and social awareness. At their best, they are the moral geniuses of a society: Gandhi, Martin Luther King, Jr., Albert Schweitzer. The human community needs these representatives of solar conscience.

The next mythical father in this Greek line of development is Zeus. When Zeus comes to dominate solar conscience, we find once again aspects of repression (Zeus locks the Titans up in Tartaros) and child-devouring (he swallows Metis, who is pregnant with his child, later born from his head as Athena). But the reign of Zeus also demonstrates much greater flexibility: he allows for the play of both good and evil within his kingdom, and he tolerates disagreement

on Olympus. The meanings and images of Zeus in the structure of solar conscience will be left for the fourth chapter,
where I will discuss him in light of his primordial marriage
to Themis, an aspect of lunar conscience, to which I now turn.

Chapter Three

LUNAR CONSCIENCE

Is it possible that a bad conscience, which can literally kill people or drive them mad, is a product of nature as well as of culture? An affirmative answer would concur with a widely held conviction that we can bring lethal physical and mental illness upon ourselves by behaving badly. Guilt is not the only punishment of a bad conscience.

This view accommodates the ancient notions of Fate and Nemesis. The perception that moral values are carried forward not only by culture but also by human nature itself is an idea with ancient roots. Perhaps the human psyche is constructed in such a way that ethical sensitivity is at least partially inherited.

I would like to put forward the notion that solar conscience is the source of law and the inner representative of a particular society's laws, while lunar conscience is the source of the perception of justice, a deeper sense of right and wrong that does not depend upon or reflect the "common law," that transcends the commonly received rules and regulations that govern a specific society. While it is necessary to retain a note of skeptical caution about all of this for the sake of rigor, the questions raised are worthy of discussion.

The tragic story of the ancient Greek house of Atreus makes the point that an evil act in one generation affects all the descendants, even to the extent of threatening the genetic line with extinction. Similarly, the idea of original sin in Christian doctrine holds that a sinful act of disobedience in the mythic past on the part of Adam and Eve has set the entire human race on a tragic course. These age-old beliefs and perceptions about crime and punishment open a vista on the subject of conscience that stretches our habitual personalistic ways of thinking about it. Perhaps conscience is not so personal and so culture-bound after all.

As we approach conscience from the lunar angle of vision, our attention will shift from the personal and even from the cultural and social determinants of moral content to the unconscious archetypal aspects of human nature and to the body and to instinct as sources of moral guidance and values. Looking away from the steady certainties of right and wrong as they are often laid down by family, by society, and by collective religion, we will now consider such phenomena as the odd paradoxes of certain ethical compulsions and the inexplicable presence of unconsciously sponsored moral responses; the symptomatology of mental illness, particularly the borderline personality disorder, as a function of lunar conscience; psychosomatic illness and synchronistic catastrophe as traces of bad conscience. The idea is that living in bad faith with life, and especially with the basic patterns of human life, condemns a person or a tribe or family to a chain of consequences that Eastern tradition would call bad karma. We will also find ourselves exploring the implications of a kind of conscience that would coerce the ego not onto a narrow trail of moral perfectionism but onto the way toward wholeness and completeness. If we found in solar conscience the fruit to be love of law, here we may find traces of a lunar law of love.

In tackling this thorny question about culture and nature, the question quickly arises, to what extent are we still speaking about conscience? Is there anything in human nature, in the "mother," in the unconscious, that can go by the name of conscience? Don't values and morals have to be taught? The etymology of the word *conscience* seems to affirm this belief, for *con science* means "knowing together"— or that which is generally known in a group's consciousness and held in common among its members.

Lunar conscience, however, suggests another way of understanding the notion of togetherness, one based less exclusively within the consciousness of a group and more in a layer of the unconscious, in what Jung called the collective unconscious. Lunar conscience speaks for that which is commonly known and accepted as human, but known and accepted because it rises up from the common substrate of the deep psyche and forms a sort of collective moral common sense. Lunar conscience arises out of the archetypal patterns, those common human building blocks of the mind that constitute our human heritage as sentient beings. It will be my contention here that this layer of unconsciousness contains its own laws of behavior, and that the violation of these laws draws penalties from within the psychosomatic wholeness that is the human person.

THE CASE OF ORESTES

A paradigmatic example of lunar conscience at work occurs in the story of the ancient Greek figure, Orestes. Orestes is the son of Clytemnestra and Agamemnon. He consults the oracle of Apollo at Delphi to determine whether or not he should revenge his father, who was murdered upon returning from the Trojan War by his angry wife. She killed him in his own palace because he had sacrificed their daughter, Iphigenia, to the goddess Artemis in order to obtain favorable winds for his expedition to Troy. Apollo upholds the patriarchal law and orders the mother's execution, which Orestes proceeds to carry out. After the murder, Orestes,

according to Aeschylus, calls the chorus to hear him, and he
appeals to the sun:

> Spread it out. Stand around me in a circle and
> display this net that caught a man. So shall, not my
> father, but that great father who sees all, the Sun,
> look on my mother's sacrilegious handiwork
> and be a witness for me in my day of trial
> how it was in all right that I achieved this death,
> my mother's . . .
> (*The Libation Bearers,* 983–989)

Both Apollo, a solar deity and as such the representative of
solar conscience, and the collective attitude, as represented
by the chorus, stand firmly behind this act of violence against
the mother, encourage it and give it moral support.

After he has committed the murder, however, Orestes
feels ambivalent, even though the chorus insists he has done
his duty. The chorus seems blind to the dark figures, the
Furies, who are beginning to gather around the father-
revenger's head:

> CHORUS
> No, what you did was well done. Do not therefore
>   bind
> your mouth to foul speech. Keep no evil on your
>   lips.
> You liberated all the Argive city when
> you lopped the heads of these two snakes with one
>   clean stroke.
>
> ORESTES
> No!

Women who serve this house, they come like
    gorgons, they
wear robes of black, and they are wreathed in a
    tangle
of snakes. I can no longer stay.

CHORUS

Orestes, dearest to your father of all men
what fancies whirl you? Hold, do not give way to
    fear.

ORESTES

These are no fancies of affliction. They are clear,
and real, and here; the bloodhounds of my
    mother's hate.
(*The Libation Bearers,* 1044–1054)

The Orestes legend gives the lie to a simple view that solar conscience is the only moderator of ethical behavior. The Erinyes, or Furies, defend the rights of the mother—even a vindictive, murderous, and morally questionable one like Clytemnestra—in the teeth of Apollo, the Sun, the Argive city, and the claims of the father. They speak for conscience at a prerational level that is not dominated by the collective. In depth psychology terms, they speak from and for the unconscious.

In his historical reconstructions, the German pioneer of studies in comparative mythology, J. J. Bachofen, uncovered a feature of ancient Mediterranean societies that he called "mother right." Mother right forms a set of obligations that arise out of the infant–mother bond. The mother–child relationship, he claimed, created the matrix out of which grows "all culture . . . every virtue . . . every nobler aspect of existence. . . . it operates in a world of violence as the divine principle of love, of union, of peace" (1954, p. 91). Bachofen laid the historical and collective foundation for what Robert Scholl (see chapter two) observes in the interactions between mother and infant when he postulates the origin of conscience in this interpersonal matrix.

The mother, earlier than the father, extends her interest beyond the ego, said Bachofen, as she contains her children in a circle of protective love. Her self-interest is extended to them, and this creates the first instance of human empathy. The nature of the maternal principle is different in many respects from the paternal principle, and here Bachofen stated a definition that can also serve as a basic distinction between lunar and solar conscience:

> Whereas the paternal principle is inherently restrictive, the maternal principle is universal; the paternal principle implies limitation to definite groups, but the maternal principle, like the life of nature, knows no barriers. The idea of motherhood produces a sense of universal fraternity among all men. . . . (1954, p. 80)

Whereas solar conscience makes distinctions, divides, elevates, judges, and excludes, lunar conscience blurs such distinctions to include, to connect, to embrace.

The matriarchal phase of cultural development, Bachofen continued, "is entirely subservient to matter and to the phenomena of natural life." It both fosters materialistic values such as bodily comfort and adornment and remains open to the more transcendent experience of "the harmony of the universe." It is "rooted in the feeling of nature," concretistic and matter-centered, yet it is also resonant to the deeper harmonies of natural existence. "In a word," Bachofen concluded, "matriarchal existence is regulated naturalism" (1954, pp. 91–92).

Whether historical research confirms or denies Bachofen's hypotheses, his reconstruction offers, in historical terms and metaphors, an account of the sources, contents, and dynamic workings of lunar conscience.

It is this aspect of conscience that Orestes unwittingly violates when he slays his mother at the recommendation of solar Apollo. The Furies, according to Hastings in his *Encyclopedia of Religions and Ethics,* are "not inner monitors, but external agencies punishing the individual for violations of the moral law," and in Aeschylus they are invisible to the chorus, which represents the collective opinion and values of the polis. Both of these points indicate the psychological distance of lunar conscience from ego values and collective consciousness: the Furies, guardians of mother right, do not belong to the world of diurnal consciousness, as represented in Greek drama by the chorus; they arise suddenly and spontaneously out of the unknown background of unconsciousness and attack the apparently guilt-free ego with their awful howling and ghastly, otherworldly appearance. Unlike solar conscience, which makes its presence known in those who err by producing feelings of guilt and separation from the warmth of family and community or a sense of moral inferiority, lunar conscience asserts its presence in madness, in bad dreams and nightmares, in feelings of persecution and anxiety that one's life is at the mercy of dark, sinister, irrational forces. This is the clinical picture of the borderline personality (see Schwartz-Salant 1989).

The origin of the Erinyes (also called Furies and sometimes apotropaically Eumenides—"the benevolent ones") tells much about their nature and function. Several myths exist. In the best known, the Erinyes come into being when Gaia is impregnated by the blood of the emasculated Uranus (Kerenyi 1988, p. 21). In another myth, they are the daughters of Night; in yet another, their mother is Earth and their father Skotos, "Darkness" (ibid., p. 47). In all accounts, they are extremely ancient, they have close genetic connections to the primordial Mother, and they occupy a place in the underworld. In Orphic belief, Hades is their father and Persephone their mother, and this view most specifically locates them among the shades (ibid.).

In the Erinyes, the Great Mother archetype gives expression to her aroused instinct for the preservation of life and especially of kinship bonds. Whenever the laws of blood kinship (the primary bond within the matriarchal world) are violated, the Erinyes appear with their stench, their "poisonous slaver," and their ferocious barking as the hounds of hell (ibid., pp. 47–48). They seem to be especially sensitive to violations of the bond to the mother.

As guardians of kinship, the Erinyes indicate a basic intention within lunar conscience: to defend the rights and prerogatives of attachment to persons, places, and material objects. Lunar conscience is based on attachment values. It is much less abstract than solar conscience. Its movement is "downward," rather than "upward," toward and into *materia* and the claims of *materia* upon the ego. It defends our intimate and pervasive feelings of attachment, our early physical and psychological bonds of relationship to people and things, and also our bond to our own body and physical need. Lunar conscience takes the attitude a mother takes toward her children: she tends to their physical need, she loves them unconditionally, emotionally, primitively, absolutely. As a mother would, lunar conscience recommends that the ego accept life and live it fully. There is imprinted in lunar conscience an ethic of acceptance and of self-acceptance.

The Furies raise their intolerable stink when the ego's primordial kinship to the mother is transgressed. And should the ego embark upon the hubris of severing or ignoring its ties to this conservative, earthbound principle in the unconscious, the Erinyes come on with the full force of their underworldly fury.

LUNAR CONSCIENCE AS
THE LAW OF NATURE

The extreme age attributed to the Erinyes by Aeschylus and other ancient authorities indicates not only their primordial historical origins among prehistoric populations but also the psychological primacy and primitiveness of their activities and values. Their great age places the origin of lunar conscience beyond or before the consolidation of the ego and the formation of other complexes. Lunar conscience is an earlier form of conscience than solar conscience. Since it often works not through psychological phenomena like feelings of remorse or guilt but through bodily reactions and symptoms, its roots must be located in the sympathetic nervous system, that vast ocean of unconsciousness over which the ego has little or no control and which is, in a sense, the "mother" of the ego.

Constantin von Monakow speaks of a "biological conscience," calling it by the Greek name *syneidesis. Syneidesis,* he says, is deeply rooted in every living, organized protoplasm (1950, p. 264). Its function is to ensure orderly process and development or, to use a phrase of Jung's, "to conserve the possibilities of life" (1950, p. 337n). It exists, writes Monakow, "to insure the future interests of the individual and the race" (1950, p. 249). This intuition of the basis of conscience even beyond the mother–infant bond in the natural order itself—forming a kind of natural ground plan on which the life of an individual member of the species must rest—lies at the heart of our theme and will be further developed in discussions of such mythic figures as Themis, Dike, and Maat. To live according to and within the limits of this plan becomes, in the light of Luna, a matter of conscience.

Some of the ways in which one suffers when one departs from or violates this basic ground plan of life are told by various inflictions which the Erinyes bring upon their victims and by their several instruments of torture. One hallmark of their presence is the "drivenness" of the victim: like Orestes wandering the earth, for years dodging and fleeing, so a person who is forever restless, suffering from compulsive dissatisfactions with place and situation and a constant need to change because of anxiety and fear, given to paranoid uneasiness, signals punishment by lunar conscience. In this constant movement there is plenty of desperation, and great speed is required, for the Furies are winged.

Insanity and illness (psychosomatic and hypochondriacal) also threaten. In myth, the Furies are blamed for sickness, disease, madness, and death. Their stench and horrendous appearance imply paroxysms of self-loathing, which induces frantic flight out of oneself into avenues of escape of every sort. Their whips and red-hot irons lacerate the flesh and raise livid welts as they go about their devilish work of castigation and destruction.

All of this morbid symptomatology notwithstanding, the purpose of the Erinyes is to protect mother right, and so the symptoms are meant not only to punish but to further a teleological aim as well. They are meant to remind the victim of bad lunar conscience of the law of kinship, attachment, concrete relatedness.

The implacable hostility of the Erinyes extends, in the opinion of Roscher, to include the cardinal sin of Greek culture, hubris (pp. 1321–1323). Hubris was to the ancient Greeks what disobedience was to the ancient Hebrews, an act of ultimate defiance that held enormously far-reaching implications and subtle dimensions. At its core is the act of overstepping a boundary that has been laid down by the gods: hubris means forgetting that one is human and not divine. It is archetypal inflation. While hubris is sometimes punished by the Erinyes (specifically for violations of mother right and family right), such punishment more often falls to their cousin, Nemesis.

Like the Erinyes, Nemesis, whose name means "righteous anger," is a winged daughter of Night. Her wrath "is directed against those who have violated order, especially the order of nature, and have disregarded nature's law and norm" (Kerenyi 1988, p. 105). Upon such persons she wreaks havoc, bringing low the mighty and deflating the puffed-up. To her falls the task of keeping humans from demeaning the gods and aggrandizing themselves, or, when they do so, to destroy them utterly. The disasters and tragedies that befall us because of hubris are the work of Nemesis, and she serves to put us back in touch with human proportion and modesty—sometimes by causing us to stumble, or in horrific dreams, or by instilling irrational fears of failing, or by inaugurating a giveaway nervous twitch that mars the appearance of aplomb and perfection. The righteous anger of Nemesis attacks hubris and defends nature's law and norm.

Lunar conscience is, in this respect, markedly conservative, a chief function of it being to say "no" to the ambitions of an ego that seeks ever to depart from its linkages and many attachments to earth and nature. Whereas solar conscience is full of what one ought to do and seeks to coerce the ego into falling in line with an ideal image, lunar conscience is occupied largely with inhibitions. The daimon of Socrates, a classical instance of lunar conscience, spoke only to inhibit, never to urge on. The "still, small voice" of lunar conscience speaks in moments of reflection, as one searches for a sense of proportion and for an intuition of act or word that fits the basic plan, the gestalt of the moment and the pattern of the whole life. Lunar conscience tells us when that word or act does not match up, when it oversteps or violates. All the bizarre and freakish symptoms—the work of Nemesis and the Erinyes—scream to call us back, to take note, to remind the ego that it cannot do whatever it pleases, or even whatever Apollo might will.

That the Erinyes speak out of "absolute knowledge" of a person's destiny is argued in myth by their relation, through their mother, Night, to the Moirai, the Fates, over whose decisions even Zeus himself can exercise no veto.

THE POSITIVE VALUES
OF LUNAR CONSCIENCE

The Erinyes are not the total sum and substance of lunar conscience. They represent the "dark side of the moon," the punishments of bad conscience. They are in lunar conscience what the devouring father is in solar conscience. What in lunar conscience corresponds to the "good father" of solar conscience is found in symbols of order and justice that pertain to the natural world. As the solar side of the moral archetype extracts the moral factor from the spiritually based archetypes, so the lunar side extracts the moral factor from the materially based instincts. This is then mediated via the function of lunar conscience through to the ego. Through the lunar aspect of conscience, nature speaks.

Bachofen's construction of three stages of cultural development offers a pattern that is relevant to understanding lunar conscience. In his view, human society began with a "hetaeric stage." This was characterized by "unbridled instinctuality," in which the strongest members of the horde took food, shelter, sexual gratification, and other desirable items for themselves. Love, order, justice, consideration for others, a tradition of ethical conduct were entirely unknown.

Women, in order to defend themselves, were forced into sexual servitude.

The transformation of this hetaeric stage into the matriarchal stage was initiated by the love that sprang up between mothers and children:

> At the lowest, darkest stages of human existence the love between mother and her offspring is the bright spot in life, the only light in the moral darkness, the only joy amid profound misery. (Bachofen 1954, p. 79)

Mothers were the first to breach the purely egoistic attitude of humankind and to include in their circle of concern an object of love beyond themselves, a "not-I." Mother love broke the narcissistic spell and introduced object relations into the human world. As this new attitude grew and generalized, it transformed society into matriarchy, whose essential hallmarks were universal acceptance of all creatures, "regulated naturalism," and a religion based on intuitions of harmonies in the natural order.

This led to the next stage, in which the father–child relationship came into existence. This transformed culture into the patriarchal form, whose main features are modeled upon this father–child relationship: hierarchies of order (father over child, elder brother over younger, sons over daughters, leaders over followers, and so on), obedience on the part of lower creatures toward those above them, and a kind of spirituality that pits spirit against nature and strongly favors the former in the notion of ethics as an *opus contra naturam*.

I present this highly abbreviated account of Bachofen's fascinating theory, which is still very relevant to contemporary discussions about gender and possible utopias, in order to consider the moral factor that comes into being as culture moves from the hetaeric to the matriarchal pattern. Beginning with the highly specific, personal relationship between mother and child, out of which non–self-seeking or agapic love is born, this development of attitude generalized, according to Bachofen, to take into account the whole of humanity and the natural world. It achieves, in short, a level of transcendence that does not separate the person from roots in the natural world but rather "sees through" the empirical world, as it were, to a level that holds the multiplicity of natural phenomena ("the many") in the arms of unity ("the one"). Here we see the "horizontal transcendence" of lunar conscience, as opposed to the "vertical transcendence" of solar conscience.

A dream illustrates this. A young man, whose conscious attitude leaned heavily toward vertical transcendence, with a strong sense of solar conscience, had the following dream, which was compensatory to his conscious situation and made a strong impact on him.

> I am in a large auditorium, sitting in the front row and awaiting the appearance of the guest speaker, an Indian guru. Finally, he comes on stage. He points to a picture that is rectangular and more horizontal than vertical by a proportion of perhaps two-to-one. It is a landscape—a house set amidst some mountains and trees. The house, mountains, clouds, trees are all made up of one continuous line.
>
> The speaker asks the audience what this picture means, and he invites speculation. When no one comes up with an adequate response, he says all of the objects in the picture are "joined" like that because "love joins everything in the universe."

This perception of linkage among all things—natural objects as well as cultural artifacts—through Eros is the basis of the fundamental moral principle of lunar conscience. All things are joined.

Several mythological figures, all of them feminine and connected intimately to the matriarchal mythic and cultural world, image the archetypal pattern of horizontal transcendence that undergirds lunar conscience. The first I will consider is the Greek goddess Themis.

The myth of Themis is the myth of lunar conscience. Themis is the daughter of Gaia and Uranus, according to Hesiod (*Theogony* 135). She belongs, therefore, to the pre-Olympian world of the Titans, of which only Themis and Leto appear later among the Olympians. According to Roscher, her name means "that which is set, placed." A closely related word, *themeley,* is the name given to the earth as solid ground. "The earth," writes Roscher, "is here not seen as provider of nourishment (Demeter), nor as the goddess of the deeps (as in its death aspect), but in the sense of solidity, immovability" (1924–1937). Thus, while she is often considered to be an earth goddess and sometimes even identified with Gaia, as when Aeschylus has Prometheus say ". . . she that was my mother, Themis, Earth—she is but one although her names are many . . ." (*Prometheus Bound,* 209–210), Themis does not represent *materia* itself but a quality of earth, namely its stability, solidity, immovability. These connections of Themis to the earth and to the Titanic world bespeak the solidity and conservatism of lunar conscience, its roots in ancient and stable patterns and processes.

Of particular importance for my thesis here is the mantic aspect of Themis: she is a goddess who speaks to humans through oracles. The most famous of all oracular locations in ancient Greece, Delphi, belonged originally to Gaia, who passed the site to her daughter Themis. After that it went to Phoebe, and only in the end was it inhabited by Apollo. Jane Harrison argues, however, that Themis is the oracular principle itself, so that instead of there being four stages of possession at Delphi, there are only three—Gaia-Themis,

Phoebe-Themis, and Apollo-Themis (1912, p. 382). In other words, Themis is most essentially about the business of oracle-giving, and at bottom she represents the oracular mouth of the earth, the voice of nature herself. Themis is Earth speaking.

"The light from the tripod . . . shown through the bosom of Themis onto Parnassus," writes Plutarch, thus attesting to Themis's central role at Delphi (in Harrison 1912, p. 389). Roscher surmises that Themis was originally "a chthonic prophetess, a representative of the unchangeable laws of the firm earth, her mother." Harrison claims that the oracles given by Themis were not prophesies in the sense of predictions of future events, but rather *Themistes* or "ordinances" (p. 387). These ordinances would be the "laws of nature" as they applied to humankind.

The succession at Delphi from Gaia through Themis and Phoebe to Apollo tells of a transition from earth oracle (Gaia-Themis) through moon oracle (Phoebe-Themis) to sun oracle (Apollo). We see here not only the development from matriarchy to patriarchy, but also a movement from the predominance of lunar conscience to the rule of solar conscience. Orestes, it should be noted, went to Delphi with his original moral predicament and received instructions from Apollo to murder his mother, an act which aroused the furious Erinyes (lunar conscience) to exact such a dear price of suffering from him.

Other myths also tell of conflict between Gaia-Themis and Apollo at Delphi, and the cleft between them seems never to have been finally bridged. One story tells of Gaia's anger and jealousy upon the succession of Apollo. To compete with and thwart the Apollonic divinations, she "sent up dreams for the guidance of mortal men in their cities" (Farnell 1907, vol. 3, p. 9).

Euripides mentions this myth in "Iphigenia in Taurus," a play which tells of the resolution of Orestes' trials. The poet's dramatic rendition of the conflict between Apollo and Themis, and ultimately between matriarchal and patriarchal powers, throws into high relief the contrast between the two systems, the one with oracles and dreams, and the other with "lips of light":

The Third Maiden
But Earth had wished to save the oracle
    For Themis, Her own daughter,
And so in anger bred a band of dreams
Which in the night should be oracular
    To men, foretelling truth.
And this impaired the dignity of Phoebus
    And of His prophecies.

The Second Maiden
And the baby God went hurrying to Zeus,
Coaxed with His little hands and begged of Zeus
    To send the dreams away.

The First Maiden
And Zeus was very pleased to have His Son
Come straight to Him with troubles. His great brow
    Decided with a nod
That Phoebus have his prize restored to Him,
    In spite of angry Earth,
His throne, His listening throng, His golden voice . . .

The Fourth Maiden
The throats of night be stricken straightaway mute
    And plague mankind no more,
That shapes of night no longer hold their power

To foretell truth in syllables of gloom
  And haunt men's aching hearts—
That men be freed from the prophetic dark
  And every shrouded form
And listen only to the lips of light.
(lines 1259–1284)

In this mythic account we see clearly the deep separation between the way of the earth with her pits and abysmal valleys and dark holes and the way of the sky with its brightness and lucid clairvoyance. This is a separation that widened even further into a split in Western culture and religion and can be studied in the Gnostic-Christian controversies, in the relationship between alchemy and Christian orthodoxy, and in the modern tensions between depth psychology and traditional religion (see Stein 1985).

Keeping in mind these connections of Themis to Gaia and to Delphi, we must now consider her central and most important attribute, justice. The meaning of the word *Themis,* Vos asserts in her entry on Themis in the *Bibliotheca Classica Vangorcumiana,* was always "right" and never merely custom, commandment, or decree. Themis speaks for a natural order and law that precedes culturally conditioned notions of organization and the rules derived from society's needs.

In the view of those thinkers who are more or less persuaded of the sociological origins of all human knowledge and attitudes, Themis would be seen as an abstraction of human notions of justice that developed through the interactions of humans in a specific culture, presumably a matrifocal one. An alternative, archetypal view would hold that Themis is not a product of social organization but the presupposition for such if such there ever was, that her psychological existence precedes and underlies humanity's understanding of what she means or what she will teach. The archetypal view would locate her origin in psychic nature, in the collective unconscious, rather than in culture and collective consciousness. She is not derivative but fundamental.

Farnell's argument seems persuasive:

> Themis, as a personality in Greek religion, was originally an emanation from Ge . . . [I should like to point out] the improbability of the only other conceivable theory, that Themis began her religious career as the mere personification of the abstract idea of righteousness. Such personified abstractions are doubtless early in the religious thought of the Greeks as of other races. But the careful study of these in Greek cult and literature leads to the conviction that only those became prominent and of a certain validity in the popular religion which had emanated originally from concrete personal deities. . . . Now Themis, in the earliest literature is a very concrete figure, a living and active power in the Titanic and Olympian world. (1907, vol. 3, p. 13)

Moreover, the existence of Themis cults—in which, as Farnell points out, "mysteries" or *orgia* ("orgies") were celebrated much as they were in the Gaia cults—lends authority to the view that she is a genuine goddess and not a "mere personification of the abstract idea of righteousness."

As a goddess, Themis is a psychic power that speaks for Nature; she is "the oracular power of Earth," to use Harrison's fine phrase (1912, p. 480). This development of "natural ethics," of a kind of natural righteousness, out of the Great Mother finds further mythical confirmation in other feminine deities, notably in Adrasteia.

Farnell surmises that Adrasteia was probably a local title for Cybele, the Great Mother goddess of Asia Minor. A mountain goddess, she was attended by the Idaean Dactyls (dwarfs) and was given the epithet, "the goddess from whom one cannot run away." For this reason, she was often associated with Nemesis (Farnell 1907, vol. 2, p. 499). Her name can mean also "the inescapable" (Kerenyi 1988, p. 91). In Orphic tales, Adrasteia sits before the cave, and "with the tones of brazen drum . . . she held men in the spell of justice" (ibid., p. 115). The linkages between Adrasteia and Nemesis pass over also to Themis, for aroused by evil Themis turns into Ichnaia, a goddess who, like Adrasteia and Nemesis, fiercely searches out evil with sharp eyes and brings destruction down upon the heads of evildoers. The sword is a symbol of Themis: it is the sword of nature's justice.

But who are the wicked in nature's eyes? The prime offense against Themis, the quality that for her defines the essence of evil, is hubris. According to Vos, Themis and hubris represent polar opposites: where Themis is absent there is hubris, and where Themis is present there is no hubris. Themis speaks for and defends the "ground plan," humanity's rootedness in an unshakable natural order, while hubris is "no plan," the denial of humanity's place in nature and of the superiority of the gods, the willful humanization of gods and apotheosis of persons. Hubris gets the proportions wrong and denies the limitations that attachments imply.

Speaking for Earth, Themis defines humanity and its limitations. Her most ardent adversary on Olympus is Ares, the god of war whose appetite for strife and whose blood lust know no bounds. Not that Themis is invariably opposed to war either; she is not a pacifist. In fact, she encourages Zeus to unleash the forces that produce the Trojan War, but she does so on environmental grounds: it will reduce the human population! As a rationale, this is typical of her concern for distribution, proportion, and the resources of the earth.

Her implacable opposition to the evil of human hubris has a further significance for the deeper meanings of Themis.

74

As the mother of the Horae (the seasons or hours), Themis stands behind the orderly progression of time in nature. The Horae represent the natural orderliness of the cosmos: winter turning to spring, day to night, one hour to the next. Human beings also are subject to time. Like the changing seasons, and the sun's passage through the sky, and the moon waxing and waning, humans pass through a life cycle: they are born, they grow from infants to children to adults, and in the end they die. The gods do not, they are immortal.

These stages of life are fixed in length and determined by another set of goddesses behind Themis, the Fates. When we think of human life developmentally as a series of stages, we participate in Themis's viewpoint: tasks required in one stage may not be recommended in another because they do not "fit." The "rightness" of an attitude or action may vary according to which stage a person happens to occupy. The attitudes and actions that connote the puer, for example, and belong appropriately to adolescence are grossly out of tune in the psychology of a middle-aged man (see von Franz 1981). Correct timing, therefore, is a part of Themis's sense of rightness and justice. Humans pass through developmental stages, and attitudes are not fixed and of permanent validity as are the laws of righteousness as seen from the viewpoint of solar conscience.

While the principle of natural order espoused by Themis is as steady as the earth itself, her specific injunctions are changeable, like the moon. Hubris goes wrong by reversing this: the principle of natural order is ignored and instead of it a specific attitude or ego idealization assumes rigid permanency. Hubris ignores the life situation. The *puer aeternus* who is middle-aged therefore violates Themis and pays for this with his personal catastrophes. For Themis, the fundamental ground plan of the life cycle is of essential consequence; to ignore it or depart from it is hubris and calls for penalty.

The names of the three Horae also tell of their significance. Eunomia means "Lawful Order," Eirene means "Peace," and Dike means "Just Retribution." Of special interest is Dike, and what Harrison says about Dike is relevant to our theme. She writes that Dike

> is the individual way of life appropriate to each natural thing, each plant, each animal, each human being. It is also the way of that great animal, the Universe, as this is made manifest in the seasons and through the life and death cycle of vegetation. When it becomes evident that these cycles of nature depend upon the movements and influences of heavenly bodies, Dike becomes manifested in the risings and settings of constellations, in the waxing and waning of the Moon, and in the daily and yearly course of the Sun. (Harrison 1912, p. 517)

Humanity as a whole is therefore included in Dike's natural way, and through Dike humans are linked to the rest of the natural cosmos. As the glue of the universe, Dike represents the inner connectedness of things, while at the same time she represents the individual essence of each thing as it naturally is in itself. Each has its own natural way, and all together they make up a cosmos, which has its natural way as a whole.

For animals, this amazing connection between the one and the many apparently poses no great dilemma: each one lives according to its own nature, and this fortuitously works out as a part of the Dike of the whole cosmos. But for humans, this poses a problem that goes to the heart of the ethical question: should I fulfill my own individual way at the cost of others, or should I sacrifice myself and my individuality for the sake of others or in order to adapt to the group?

And should humankind as a whole sacrifice certain drives and gratifications for the sake of the natural order?

Solar conscience, with its traditions and experience and sure knowledge of right and wrong is inclined to rush in with answers to such questions. With lunar conscience, the answers come more slowly. In large measure, humanity has lost the knowledge of what a natural way is and, in the process, has become deafened to the voice that nature and instinct might release. Themis and Dike elucidate the ethical side of instinct, the still, small voice within the drive or impulse, the bodily reaction that inhibits, that says "no" to the reflexes of raw instinct. Themis speaks for the same thing that Dike represents, from within the earth. But since the succession of Apollo, her voice has become muted and much less clear, appearing, according to myth, only in dreams. And to follow the path laid down by dreams is, as we students and practitioners of modern depth psychology know, a task of immense difficulty, loaded with pitfalls and uncertainties.

The Dike of humanity, its natural way, for which Themis is the speaker, is an instinctually based function, much akin to what Jung calls the instinct for reflection:

> Ordinarily we do not think of "reflection" as ever having been instinctive, but associate it with a conscious state of mind. *Reflexio* means "bending back" and, used psychologically, would denote the fact that the reflex which carries the stimulus over into instinctive discharge is interfered with by psychization. Owing to this interference, the psychic processes exert an attraction on the impulse to act excited by the stimulus. Therefore, before having discharged itself into the external world, the impulse is deflected into an endopsychic activity. *Reflexio* is a turning inwards, with the result that, instead of an instinctive action, there ensues a succession of derivative contents or states which may be termed reflection or deliberation . . . Through the

reflective instinct, the stimulus is more or less wholly transformed into a psychic content . . . a natural process is transformed into a conscious content. (1937, par. 241–243)

The reflective instinct breaks the stimulus–response link, and in the interval of this interruption the human being has the opportunity to see a situation consciously. By reflecting on an event, a person transforms it into psychological experience.

By the rule of lunar conscience, this reflective act and the consequent psychization of the instinct in themselves already constitute a moral act, for this partakes of the Dike of humans: it is being true to human nature to reflect. The moon, in addition to being a light in the darkness, has typically been regarded as a symbol of reflection (Cirlot 1991). Lunar conscience reflects upon and out of instinct and experience.

Hubris is impulsive and rests upon the absence of reflection. When Ulysses taunts the Cyclops—that classic example of hubris—he acts spontaneously and foolishly, without reflecting on the possible consequences of his act. In an act of hubris, the ego acts impulsively or out of an unconscious fantasy, while the instinct to reflect works for exactly the opposite result, to contain the impulse and to give it psychological body. What made the barbarians barbaric in the eyes of the Greeks, writes Vos, was the absence of Themis among them: they lacked a sense of what is fitting and proper for humans, the sense of proportion that grows out of deep and constant reflection. Therefore, they have no order and no peace. Reflection is meant to deflate one's overestimation of oneself, to hold one fast to a true image of one's place in the natural order, to keep the proportions right and just and human.

If lunar conscience is to give persons a true image of themselves and of their place in nature, however, it must have some independence, a source of power to correct the false images that egos crave for themselves. It cannot simply mirror back the ego's own image of itself, or it would merely confirm the ego in hubris. Like the queen's mirror in the fairy tale of Snow White, lunar conscience as mirror must possess the capacity for truth-telling. This kind of reflection cannot therefore be merely an act of casuistic reflection within ego-consciousness, for such reflections tend either to confirm the image of the ego by offering rationalizations or to measure it against the idealisms of solar conscience. The corrective mirror of Luna presents itself to us, rather, in dreams, active imagination, intuition, and vision.

Dreams, as Jung pointed out in many writings, are a product of nature. They are manufactured by the ego, but the ego cannot program or control them. Culture is also helpless to control dream life. Moreover, the relation of dreams to ego-consciousness is compensatory, that is, they fill in the picture, present the other side, and thus play the role of a mirror of truth, reflecting back to waking consciousness not an ideal of itself or an illusory wished-for likeness of itself but an image that illuminates the dark spot, the lacunas, the shadow or the unrecognized potential. The dream-maker, unconscious and autonomous, has a point of view that the ego not only cannot generate or control but is even unaware of. The dream is the matrix from which Gaia (and Themis, who is her oracular persona) speaks from "the far side," from within nature to "mortal men in their cities."

In some accounts, Dike belongs to the realm of Hades, to the unconscious, and from there represents "the way of the whole world of nature" (Harrison 1912, pp. 516, 521).

TWO DREAMS

Two contemporary dreams from the case of an analysand illustrate lunar conscience at work in modern form. This discussion is not meant to exhaust the meaning of these dreams but to indicate a number of motifs that are strikingly present in the myth, too.

The dreamer, a thirty-year-old American man, had for some time suffered from depressive moods and self-doubts that were more or less directly related to a task (Herculean in proportion, as he saw it) awaiting him in the coming year. He had to move and change jobs, and as the date approached he realized ever more keenly the depth of his attachments to his present home and to the values and life-style typical of that region. The move also meant a transition from the familiar world of a less formal student life into the less familiar realities of the professional world with more demanding challenges and sharper competition among peers. After a particular analytical session, he saw his moods and resistances to leaving as a function of his mother complex and his longing to remain in childhood and dependent on others. At that moment, he decided to put away his childishness and face life "like a man." Psychologically, this for him meant killing his mother (complex).

That night he had the following dream:

> My mother has suddenly and unexpectedly died. I go into the room where she is lying. The undertaker has made her up so that I can hardly recognize her. Suddenly she moves an arm, then she mumbles some crazy words and waves her hand about as she tries to sit up. I'm amazed at this but figure it's some excess of energy draining out of the brain, not real life. The next day, I receive in the mail some of her effects; this seems to indicate the finality of her death.

The analysand interpreted this dream positively, seeing in it the effect of his conscious decision upon the mother complex. He experienced no guilt or remorse, although he was somewhat disturbed by the grotesque imagery of the dream and by its nightmarish quality.

This dream was followed two nights later by a truly frightening nightmare:

> My wife and I are with our son in the home of some friends. We prepare to leave, gather up many belongings, and together we go out of the house. Suddenly I realize that I've forgotten some things inside and return alone to fetch them.
>
> When I come to the door again on my way out, I see my wife running frantically up and down, beside herself with terror. I ask what's wrong and she points to a nearby tree. There I see my son sitting high on a branch; beside him sits a large black bird, and the bird is pecking at his eyes. The child cries but is helpless. In desperation I pick up a stone and throw it at the bird, but the stone strikes my son on the foot, knocking him off balance. He tumbles backwards out of the tree and is caught by people standing below. I take him up and examine him for injuries; all I can find is a red spot near his left eye where the bird had begun his work. Now I am overcome by anxiety at the risk I have taken in throwing the stone, for I could have injured my son with it; but I had no choice. I awake in a state of anxiety and fright.

The opening of the dream describes the dreamer's situation: leaving the home of friends and gathering up many belongings as he does so. The friends happened to be a family that had settled permanently in this area. This task of gathering up possessions (psychologically, the need to take the "values" away with you when you leave a place) is followed by a dramatization of the situation which indicates the profound dangers inherent in this act of moving.

The child in a tree is a widespread archetypal symbol of the mother–child relationship. The mother, who had seemingly died in the previous dream, is here transformed into a tree. This is the Great Mother in her vegetative aspect, which reaches down into the lowest depths of the unconscious and touches upon the psychoid, matter-bound side of reality. The dreamer's conscious attitude of "decision against this childishness" and the consequent "death of the mother" in the first dream has touched off a reaction from the collective unconscious and constellated an archetypal situation.

The sinister bird (which the dreamer later described as something dark and evil) lives in this tree and represents a highly threatening animus of the mother that attacks specifically the left eye of the child. This bird corresponds to the ancient Erinyes, and the entire dream, a shocking nightmare, represents an invasion of the defenders of mother right, who proceed to attack the Orestes-like ego position of the dreamer.

There are many symbolic and historical connections between the left eye and the principle of Eros. Whereas the right eye represents diurnal consciousness—dividing, separating, distinguishing—the left eye connects, joins, attaches. The left side in general connects us to the "abysmal side of bodily man," to materiality and corporality, to the slow changing of the lunar world, which will not release attachments or allow one to move on overnight. The left eye thus represents consciousness of the abysmal side, a view of life through the moon rather than through the sun, awareness of the many sticky attachments one has formed to the objects and values of one's immediate physical surroundings. The dream as a whole functions to shock the dreamer into taking note of the danger into which he has fallen.

"Saving the child" is a central concern of lunar conscience. Here the maternal instinct intrudes and asserts its priority. At all costs and for whatever risks may be necessary, the child must be restored to safety and protected. Slaying the mother, and with her the maternal principle, has the consequences of threatening the child, of robbing life of its Eros attachments, inconvenient and messy as these often seem to consciousness, and of constellating the furious reprisals of the negative mother in the form of the Erinyes. Rather than inflicting its vengeance on the ego in the forms of guilt and remorse, as is the case with solar conscience, lunar conscience devastates through nightmares, phobias, psychosomatic symptoms. The defense against this attack of lunar conscience is a kind of schizoid adulthood that finds itself hopelessly split and separated from Eros, from human warmth, from attachments to *materia,* and plagued by invisible enemies in the night.

Dreams, as well as visions and intuitions, which are all products of the unconscious mind, have the function of mediating between individuals and their Dike, their natural way. Jung's technique of active imagination follows this road. His insistence on the active part of active imagination, as well as his emphasis on the need to take dreams with the utmost ethical seriousness, represent an attempt to integrate lunar conscience into waking life as fully as possible. This integration results in a sort of binocular vision, looking at life situations from both sides at once, with both right and left eyes.

What happens if the ego fails to respond with sufficient moral seriousness to these promptings of nature? Nature passes judgment: the dreams show regression and turn into nightmares, the Erinyes and Nemesis are constellated, Themis turns into Ichnaia, and Dike's "just retribution" becomes nature's revenge. In short, when lunar conscience judges and condemns, the punishment tends less often to be a guilt reaction within consciousness than a physical reaction or a synchronistic event. The unconscious, it seems, can become violently agitated, and this produces catastrophes of many sorts—moods, compulsions, neurosis, psychosomatic maladies, accidents, terrible dreams, illness, and human tragedy.

MAAT

That the judgments of lunar conscience originate and occur on "the other side," so to speak, is further attested by the role of the Egyptian goddess Maat in the judgment of the dead. Maat is the Egyptian equivalent of the Greek Themis and is just as explicitly the divine representative of cosmic natural law and order. Maat, writes Budge in his monumental study of Egyptian mythology, "was the highest conception of physical and moral law and order known to the Egyptians" (1969, p. 421). Her name itself meant, according to Brandon, "truth, order, justice, right" (1967, p. 11). Her hieroglyph ◁▭ "was intended to represent some tool which was used by sculptors and carvers, e.g., a chisel"; it indicated "that which is straight" and was the instrument by which the work of craftsmen was kept on course (Budge 1969, p. 416).

Metaphorically, Maat is a "rule, or law, or canon, by which the lives of men and their actions were kept straight and governed" (ibid., p. 417). But beyond that, this goddess represented "the fundamental law of the universe," the orderliness of nature also depicted in the myths of Themis and Dike (Brandon 1967, p. 11). As the principle of cosmic order, Maat "came to be regarded as the principle of social order, finding expression in justice, truth and righteousness. . . . Opposed to Maat . . . was disorder" (ibid.). Here again, as in the myth of Themis, cosmic order precedes and forms the a priori condition for social order.

As cosmic order, Maat is the food of the sun-god Re; she is also the "eye of Re" and the Ka of Re (Brandon 1967, p. 11; Budge 1969, p. 418; Bonnet 1952, p. 432). She is the "lady of heaven, queen of the earth, and mistress of the Underworld" (Budge 1969, p. 418). Maat's great enemy is Set, the Egyptian version of the Greek Ares, a god of gross disorder, injustice, and ambition.

Maat's most crucial mythological activity takes place in the Hall of Two Truths (Maati), where the dead go for final judgment. Here the heart is placed on a scale against an ostrich feather, which is a symbol for Maat (truth). Sometimes Maat is herself the balance (Budge 1969). It is unclear how the scale should tip in order for the soul of the dead person to be judged just (Brandon thinks heart and feather should balance each other exactly). At any rate, if the heart weighs in correctly against the weight of Maat, the person is justified. The heart was then said to be "true of voice . . . in other words, it fitted into its allotted place in the divine order" (Ions 1965, p. 115). If not, the person was thrown to a "fearsome hybrid monster, made up of the parts of a crocodile, a lion, and a hippopotamus" named Ammut, "eater of the dead" (Brandon 1967, p. 29).

That the heart is the organ chosen to be weighed is noteworthy. To the Egyptians, writes Brandon,

> the heart was not only a vital organ of the body, it was also the conscience—in fact it was actually hypostatized as "the god which is in man." (1967, p. 37)

The heart represents, then, the voice of Maat in the human being, the oracular voice of cosmic order which breaks through into the human world.

A striking Old Testament echo to this notion is voiced by the prophet Jeremiah as he speaks for Yahweh: "I will put my law in their inward parts, and write it in their hearts" (Jer. 31:33). For the Egyptian, apparently, this was not a promise but a fact: one's heart testified for Maat!

For this same reason, however, the words of the heart became a problem for the Egyptian. The heart was autonomous and marched to its own drummer. The danger of this became especially apparent in the Hall of Two Truths, where the heart was perfectly willing to testify against the person, thus showing its much stronger affinities for Maat (truth) than for the ego. "This belief," writes Brandon,

> was so firmly established that a special prayer, addressed to the heart, was inscribed on a scarab-shaped amulet and laid on the place of the heart during the ritual of embalmment . . . it was uttered by the deceased" (1967, p. 37)

The prayer begs the heart not to rise up "as a witness against me," not to be "against me before the tribunal" (ibid.).

For the ancient Egyptian, the oracular spokesman for nature's law, located in one's own body, was presumably much closer to everyday consciousness than for the Greeks, where Gaia and Themis had been forced to retreat from Delphi into the lower worlds and from there to send messages in dreams. In Egypt, the distinction between solar and lunar conscience had not yet become apparent: while Maat speaks for the cosmic order, she is also the "eye of Re" (the solar deity), and the sons of Re sit on the thrones of Pharaoh. Thus, law and justice were united, and the arbiters of the natural order and the social order were one, united under Pharaoh and Maat. Through her oracle, the heart, laws and customs of social life were confirmed by and united with the deeper intuitions of justice.

As the kingdoms decayed and fell into decadence and disharmony, the firm truth of Maat and the testimonies of the heart came into conflict with the tangled rule of the Pharaohs. Law and justice parted company. One result of this is found in the extraordinary document, "The Conversation of a World-Weary Man with His Soul" (Jacobsohn 1968). Here the soul (Ba) confronts ego-consciousness with the folly of its ways, ways that were supported by the collective opinion of the time. In this unique instance, the judgment that ordinarily was relegated to the afterlife takes place in this world, and the ego is shown a side of truth (Maat) which is not its own and which is not mediated to it through society and law. It is an instance of lunar conscience at work in what we would today call active imagination. The Ba speaks out strongly against the suicidal impulse of the discouraged protagonist.

Like Dike, Maat represents the connectedness of things within the natural world. In the natural order there are many connections, each object is related directly or indirectly to everything else, and each thing has its fitting place. Maat connects the polarities within nature, or rather suggests their inherent connections. Ions notes that Maat represented the "balance" between the antitheses: fertile valley vs. desert, good vs. evil (1965, p. 115).

In this respect, it is important also to consider Maat's relation to Thoth, "the god of equilibrium" (Budge 1969, p. 403). Thoth and Maat are counterparts. God of the moon, Thoth is also "the master of law both in its physical and moral conceptions," and he is significantly present at the weighing of the heart, where he notes the result and passes the final verdict. He is also closely associated with the heart; his name derives from the oldest name for the ibis in Egypt, and the ibis often stands hieroglyphically for the heart (ibid., p. 402). Thoth's role as god of equilibrium is of central importance, for not only does he watch the balance during the heart-weighing ceremony, but he also arbitrates in the conflicts among the gods.

> Thoth was the conciliator, and his duty was to prevent any one god from gaining too much the upper hand and destroying the others. In fact, he had to keep these hostile forces in exact equilibrium, the forces being light and darkness, or day and night, or good and evil. (Ibid., p. 405)

LUNAR CONSCIENCE AND PLURALISM

This principle that no one god should gain a complete victory reminds us of the line spoken by Artemis in Euripides' *Hippolytus,* where she cites the law on Olympus that no god may interfere with the will of another but each must have a place. This principle represents an attempt to maintain the balance of forces in a working pluralistic system, a polytheism. To retain the integrity and prerogatives of each god in the pantheon, there must be a supraordinate principle that regulates and holds together a potentially chaotic and chaos-producing situation by enforcing a law of checks and restraints. The assumption underlying this principle is that all are necessary for the sake of the cosmos as a whole.

It is this principle that underlies the conservatism of lunar conscience. Lunar conscience would have all the archetypes live and prosper within the psychological realm, for the sake of the Whole, which is a supraordinate structure (the One). Its function is to regulate this wholeness so as to give each part its due.

Solar conscience has been passed along as a feature of a monotheistic tradition in Western culture, and it functions to support the dominant monotheistic attitude of collective consciousness. It is the basis of the legal system that we know as the common law tradition. It has within it, however, much of the power-hungry, mythic, devouring father, with the insistent pressure to exclude all other gods, as well as the value of hierarchical organization within culture and society.

Lunar conscience, on the other hand, presses for justice and balance beyond the dictates of the common law and collective consensus. It also seeks the conservation of all the possibilities of life, whatever they may be. Its primary value is wholeness and completeness rather than exclusion. Lunar conscience imposes upon the ego the duty to attain completeness rather than perfection, to save even that which is dark and inferior, from the social viewpoint, for the sake of the whole. Rather than weed out and burn up those parts for the sake of a lofty ideal, it holds out to save all the phenomena. Its goal is not especially conversion or transformation, but conservation and equilibrium. Within this cosmos, the ego, too, would have a place: not the place, but a place.

THE APPEAL OF LUNAR CONSCIENCE

The sense of duty to the principle of justice that lunar conscience insinuates into the ego is of critical importance. Without this, moral seriousness would be lacking, and the ego would be left only to suffer the consequences of its error and folly without adequate preparation. The motives the ego might find for accepting lunar conscience with ethical seriousness are at least twofold: the fear of consequences, and the positive sense of love for it. I have depicted aspects of the first at sufficient length in considering such figures as the Erinyes and Nemesis. To the second I will now turn.

One of the personal attributes of Themis, as depicted by the Greek mythographers, is her great beauty, besides the attractiveness of her dignity. Roscher mentions that pictures of her are to be compared for beauty with those of Artemis,

Leto, and Athena. Her physical attractiveness is confirmed by a myth in which Zeus pursues her in his usual intemperate way and finally marries her.

Symbols of Themis include the sword and the lamp, and also marjoram and the *pudenda muliebria* (Farnell 1907, p. 15). The meaning of marjoram here is sexual and has to do with fertility. It is mentioned in a passage from Galen, in which he describes the *arbor philosophica:* "There is a certain herb or plant, named Lunatica or Berissa, whose roots are metallic earth, whose stem is red, veined with black, and whose flowers are like those of the marjoram" (quoted by Jung 1955–1956, par. 157). This mysterious plant is, according to Jung, a moon plant, and it has to do with the fertilizing influence of Luna upon the earth. From this connection we can surmise that the association of Themis to marjoram says something about her fertility and relates her to sexuality. The association of marjoram to sexuality is stated in this verse of the lovely poem by John Skelton, "To Mistress Margery Wentworth":

> With marjoram gentle,
>   The flower of goodlihead,
> Embroidered the mantle
>   Is of your maidenhead.

Marjoram bears directly upon the other emblem of Themis, the *pudenda muliebria,* which relates Themis to fertility and sexuality in a direct and unmistakable way. Farnell suggests that there were "mysteries" or *orgia* connected with the worship of Themis. As different as the ancient Greek idea of an orgy might be from our debased notion, it did center upon rites of a sexual nature whose functions served both fertility and pleasure. As devotees of *pu-*

90

denda muliebria, the worshipers of Themis were obviously engaged in highly sexualized rituals and practices.

Here Themis is seen as exciting her devotees in an intense and libidinized way. They would be drawn to her worship and to respect for her values not only out of fear of the consequences brought down on them through neglect but out of erotically charged Eros and devotion.

Through the pattern of psychic movement that we can identify as Themis, the libido poured out in this direction by the aroused devotee also energizes a commitment to the Eros that ties together the entire cosmos. Themic Eros becomes the Eros-connectedness of things in the natural world. This is the "mystery": that Themis, who can draw on sexual energy, transforms this energy into lunar conscience, into love and care for the world, for justice and balance, for the offspring of all. As Grinnell (1973) puts it: "feminine conscience," as he terms it, at once holds Eros in check and works for its symbolical transformation, contains its extraverted movement toward sexual activity and turns it by reflection into the Eros that binds the world together.

The discharges of libido that flow between Themis and her worshipers serve not only to bind the devotee to the goddess but, passing through the goddess, to bind the devotees to each other and to the world. Here is the transition from what Bachofen called the hetaeric world to the matriarchal world. The position of Themis at the center of a group, functioning there to produce the good order that results from respect and concern for others, finds expression in her mythological roles as presider over the assembly and over the feast (Harrison 1912, p. 482). At the People's Assembly in the polis, her representative sat in the foremost seat; from there she convened the assembly, called it to order, and at the end of the meeting dissolved it. On Olympus, Themis sits at the head of the Olympian table. When the settings and food are all in place, she calls the gods to eat and then functions during the meal as a regulator of the comings and goings of the servants, of the flow of wine and dispensing of food, of the harmonious interplay of elements that combine to create the Olympian banquet.

As presider over both political meetings and the Olympian table, Themis displays the ordering effect of her dignity and justice. In this respect, she echoes the Egyptian Thoth, who also functioned as an equilibrator.

THE LUNAR ASSEMBLY AND
THE LAW OF LOVE

As an archetypal image for lunar conscience, Themis would convene and preside over what Neumann called a psychological United Nations (1969, p. 103). All the archetypal figures and forces could partake and be heard. Themis brings to the proceeding a sense of moral seriousness and obliges the great and mighty to listen conscientiously to the objections or contributions of their less prominent brothers and sisters. Moreover, while she supports the rights and prerogatives of each, she also brings each into a dialogical contact with the other and thus supports, ultimately, the whole. By containing each, she binds one to one and one to all, therein creating the order of wholeness.

So while Themis opposes the dominance of one over many, she ultimately supports unity over multiplicity, wholeness over fragmentation, integration over repression. In this holding and binding activity, Themis reveals the fundamental operative principle of lunar conscience: the law of love.

Recalling Orestes, we can now see more clearly what his crime signifies. The murder of the mother is a crime as psychological as it is social. The chorus, which speaks for the values of society, can support his act. They cannot see the onslaught of the Erinyes, however, who guard and enforce the values of mother right. Obedient to the solar injunction of Apollo, Orestes violates the fundamental premise of mother right and lunar conscience. Orestes' crime is therefore a sort of reenactment of Apollo driving the serpent from Delphi and taking it over for himself. In both cases, the oracular power of Earth is repressed, and in both also this act produces violent agitations in the heart of the Great Mother. For Apollo's usurpation, the "cities of men" are thrown into confusion and suffer a split, and for his bad advice, Orestes is driven mad, roams the earth like a beast in flight, and for years suffers the persecution of the Furies.

The end of Orestes' suffering comes about through the intervention of Athena and is coincident with the redemption of his sister Iphigenia from the barbaric foreign soil of Taurus. The sacrifice of this sister to the goddess Artemis is behind the tragedies which befall the house of Agamemnon: this was the cause of Clytemnestra's terrible anger, of her revenge on Agamemnon, and thus ultimately of her own death at the hands of her son Orestes. As expiation, Orestes must retrieve from the land of Taurus a statue of Artemis, and in performing this task with the help of his faithful friend Pylades, he brings back also his long-lost sister. It is a story of redeeming the feminine.

As this tale shows, the punishment for matricide can be escaped only by bringing the feminine soul back into the land of the living. The poignant laments of Iphigenia as she stands on the shores of Taurus and weeps for home tell of her ardent wish to return to the land of Argos. She is the lost soul of the father-determined, war-making Greek nation.

As priestess of Artemis, Iphigenia is priestess of the moon, for Artemis is a lunar divinity. "When the moon shone," writes Kerenyi, "Artemis was present, and beasts and plants would dance" (1988, p. 149). Having brought both Artemis and Iphigenia back to Greece, Orestes is also bringing back the lunar element, and for this he is finally exonerated of his crime by a vote of the Athenian Assembly, over which Themis presides. Lunar conscience is satisfied, finally, and the dreaded Furies return to their lairs.

TWO ASIDES

According to David Holt (1973), the basic moral revulsion that Marx experienced in confronting modern capitalistic society had to do with a perception of nature betrayed. As Marx saw it, the independence of money and the use of money to make money represented a radical breakup of the interdependence between humanity and nature. Now, instead of depending on nature for food and sustenance, one could rely on a purely cultural artifact, money. Marx saw this severing of the vital link between human society and nature as a diabolically immoral state of affairs that was urgently in need of correction. Marx's outrage at this modern situation, as well as that of Marxists after him, has the moral flavor of the Erinyes: drive the managers and capitalistic pigs mercilessly out of existence!

On the other hand, he urged his followers to identify with the working masses (*Lumpenproletariat*). His notion of communism, brotherhood, and solidarity among the working peoples of the world amounts to a radical modern restatement of matriarchal consciousness as described by Bachofen. Another correlation is the priority of materialism in the worldviews of both. In the Marxist ethical attitude we can see, it seems to me, lunar conscience at work, although in a highly one-sided and extreme form.

Second, I wish to note that one can draw many parallels to the Themis-Dike-Maat pattern of cosmic natural order from other cultures as well. Of the Indian dharma, for example, Heinrich Zimmer writes that it is "the divine moral order by which the social structure is knit together and sustained" (1951, p. 163). Etymologically dharma derives from "to hold, to bear, to carry" and means "that which holds together, supports, upholds" (ibid.). Dharma, he goes on, refers not only to the whole context of law and custom

> but also to the essential nature, character, or quality of the individual, as a result of which his duty, social function, vocation, or moral standard is what it is . . . Dharma is ideal justice made alive; any man or thing without its dharma is an inconsistency. There are clean and unclean professions, but all participate in the Holy Power. Hence "virtue" is commensurate with perfection in one's given role. (Ibid.)

The notion of dharma illustrates the combination of relativism and absolutism found in lunar conscience: on the one hand, "virtue" is relative to one's situation in life and determined by station and individual nature; on the other hand, dharma is the absolute principle of cosmic order. Hence, one person's virtue may be another's vice.

Harrison (1912) sees a further parallel to Themis in the Chinese notion of Tao, both representing "the way of the world." For the believer in Tao, the I Ching supplies norms for ethical conduct. From the viewpoint of solar conscience, this seems arbitrary and inconsistent, to say the least, for the I Ching "changes" its morals depending on the cosmic situation at the moment of the throw. This is situation ethics in a most radical form! The consultant of the I Ching examines not his or her own heart and motives against some ideal notion of right and wrong, but the cosmic situation. On the basis of these findings, the proper course of action is chosen. This again would be consistent with the approach of lunar conscience: convene the court, find out what are the various forces at work in the situation, let the antagonists have it out with each other, and then come to a decision as to what must be done. Psychologically, this would amount to examining the dreams, the conscious situation (in its broadest range), the complexes at work in this moment, and then, after full discussion and reflection, accept the considered result of reflection. It is a procedure utterly at odds with the authoritarian workings of solar conscience.

Chapter Four

RELATIONS BETWEEN SOLAR AND LUNAR CONSCIENCE

A philosophy professor of mine told the story of participating in a civil rights Freedom March in a southern city in the 1960s. The marchers assembled at a church and began moving through the streets peacefully, singing freedom songs and preparing for a confrontation with the city fathers on the steps of the county court house. They came to a bridge, and on the bridge waiting for the demonstrators stood helmeted policemen with cattle prods and dogs. The police chief took up a bullhorn and thundered that they were in violation of the law and unless they dispersed immediately they would be arrested and sent to jail.

The professor had never been in jail. He was a law-abiding citizen and generally did not disobey the law of the land. Here was a dilemma. Should he obey the common law or continue to listen to the cry for justice and march forward? In retrospect he confessed his fear, but this was also a moment, he said, in which he understood viscerally what Kierkegaard meant by "suspension of the ethical" in favor of "the religious."

What is the relation between duty to law and duty to justice, between a conscience that speaks for lawfulness and a conscience that demands justice? Both speak for morality of a sort, and both confront the ego with ethical imperatives. It could be argued that justice is the basis of law, but it could also be argued that justice depends upon law. Which has priority, and how can they be related within the individual and in society?

In this chapter I will examine the relationship between solar conscience and lunar conscience, two aspects of a single psychological entity that confronts the ego with demands to renounce immediate self-interest and gratification in favor of some "other." But which "other," Sol or Luna? To consult one's own personal conscience is often a murky and ambiguous matter, and clear-cut answers are usually not forthcoming.

To examine the psychological basis of solar conscience, I began by looking at the sociological or interpersonal theory that holds conscience to be fundamentally rooted in real-world authority figures and only secondarily an internal psychological factor. It becomes internal through the process of introjection, and so the voice of conscience is seen as an echo of parents and other formative authority figures. From there I went on to look at Freud's vision of a phylogenetic basis for conscience and considered his anthropological speculations about a primal horde, in which a fiercely possessive father was murdered by his dominated jealous sons, who then experienced remorse and offered sacrifices of expiation. This primal event of crime followed by internal punishment lays the groundwork for the inner persecutor we know as conscience.

Freud's image of a primal scene of incest and murder led to an examination of the Greek mythological fathers, Uranus and Kronos. Here again are mythic fathers who are anxious about their sons overthrowing them and who try to forestall that grim prospect by repressing them. They are ultimately unsuccessful: Uranus is castrated by his son, Kronos, and Kronos is thrown into Tartaros by his son, Zeus. Zeus, the heir of this lineage of gods, also shows anxiety about his position and attempts to secure it by swallowing Metis, the pregnant mother of Athena.

These myths are, I have suggested, indicative of the background or underpinnings of solar conscience. Solar conscience manifests in the psyche as a complex does: its proximity to consciousness creates anxiety. While the concrete values of solar conscience derive from external authority figures and represent the dominant moral values of family, group, and culture, it is dynamically energized, as Freud observed, by an expectation of punishment which, in many cases, has little to do with the threats of real authority figures. The severity and brutality of conscience has something strangely archaic and primitive about it. Freud's term for it, the superego, is particularly suited to solar conscience, for in its relation to the ego it stands "above," judging, insisting on rules, making boundaries and promulgating do's and don'ts. In short, it tries to bring the ego's activities and attitudes into line with particular patterns that are acceptable to the dominants of collective life. In this fashion, solar conscience is the inner speaker for the common law, the collective mores and customs of a specific social context.

Solar conscience is also instrumental in creating what Jung called the shadow. The shadow is made up of those parts of the self that are unacceptable to social life. Solar conscience polices the inner world, and the shadow figures hide from its gaze in the dark places of the psyche.

Solar conscience is also related to the ego-ideal, which stands in strong contrast to the shadow. The ego usually can maintain the illusion that it is nearly identical to the ideal, until the veil is pierced by some life event and it comes to reckon with itself more realistically. But solar conscience and the ego ideal can shine so brightly and appear so attractive that the ego positively falls in love with them, and this love affair, perhaps solar conscience's highest achievement, produces within a person the love of law. Solar conscience produces a legalistic tradition, which is also a tradition of passion.

In contrast to this excluding and idealizing trend in solar conscience, lunar conscience seeks to conserve the possibilities of life, even those which may lie in the realm of shadow. Rather than perfecting and narrowing the patterns of possible attitudes and behavior, lunar conscience insists, in the name of justice, on expanding them, on giving each archetype its due, on connecting the ego to its shadow, to the neglected child, to the host of other archetypal possibilities inherent in the fertility of the mother unconscious. This is not to say that lunar conscience represents a principle of blind tolerance, for the Furies are anything but tolerant of breaches in the code of mother right. Lunar conscience attacks and aims to destroy the rigidities and one-sided adaptations induced by solar conscience. For this reason, one is sometimes confronted by the seeming anomaly of the person who has fulfilled all duties to family and society without question, who has toed the collective line with great conscientiousness, who yet suffers the burden of a "bad conscience" for not having lived a full life. Such a person has observed solar conscience but has neglected the duty to fulfill an individual life.

From Freud's primal father through the line of mythological fathers, Uranus to Kronos to Zeus, the mythic representatives of solar conscience show themselves to be anxiously concerned about maintaining their position of authority. They are an anxious group. Out of fear of losing preeminence, the mythical fathers destroy or devour their potential rivals, usually their own children. One observes this element of anxiety not only in political leaders of collective life, whether secular or sacred, but also in the dominating super-ego of an exclusivistic, one-sided individual.

Looking through the lenses of depth psychology, the archetypal basis of ego-consciousness itself can be seen to contain a component that behaves like solar conscience: exclusivistic, insisting on one particular set of laws and guidelines, anxious to maintain its dominance over the other complexes, pressing (as in the case of Hippolytus) toward a sort of psychological monotheism. It may well be the case that there is an inherent affinity between ego development and the development of solar conscience.

Even in a matrifocal culture, therefore, insofar as individual ego development occurred or was encouraged, there would be pressure toward solar conscience. The hippy culture of the 1960s, for instance, with its antiestablishment values and irreverence for the patriarchal tradition, still had its own form of solar conscience, right down to insistence on hair length, clothing, patterns of thought and reaction, and choice of pleasure. Likewise, the extreme individualist who refuses to join any group out of principle and lives a life of grandiose inflation and isolated splendor is subject to the authority of a compulsion to be unique, which has its own solar conscience.

Any attitude characterized by rigidity and exclusiveness betrays the presence of solar conscience. Solar conscience is the voice of the one true God who will brook no rivals and countenance no equals. "Why can't everyone be like me, open, tolerant, pacifistic?" is as much a question spoken by solar conscience as is the typical paternalistic "Why can't you be like everyone else?" Both would insist on one pattern, on one law, on one mode of being in the world.

Any archetypal pattern which insists on its exclusive authority, whether over the individual ego or over the group, trumpets forth the voice of solar conscience. Solar conscience is not merely the speaker for collective values, it is the creator and enforcer of mass-mindedness and collectivity.

However, within the same psyche the lunar aspect of conscience is also at work, albeit perhaps in repressed form. Lunar conscience poses the doubt about the absolute values of the dominant pattern. It seeks to relativize, to undo the rigidities, to dissolve the exclusiveness. This work it carries out in the name of justice, justice to the other possibilities of life, to the other patterns, to the neglected archetypes which have been cast into the shadow by the dominance of one. It operates on the principle of the law of love and thus seeks to unite the many, to join the ego to all, to foster the growth of the child rather than to devour it out of fear of competition. It brings Eros into play, and Eros would join rather than separate, expand rather than narrow, flow rather than rigidify. It becomes readily apparent how Luna here works against Sol, how at odds they are with regard to their fundamental objectives. And yet, each needs the other. Law needs justice, and justice needs law. In their relationship we will find the deepest appreciation for each.

ZEUS AS SOLAR CONSCIENCE

For an insight into some of the possible relations between solar and lunar conscience, we will look at the myth of Zeus and later at his marriage to Themis. In many respects, Zeus recapitulates the patterns of his father Kronos and his grandfather Uranus. Like them, a recipient of an oracle that he will bear a son who will overthrow him, Zeus is anxious about his authority. When his first wife, Metis, becomes pregnant, he seeks to elude his fate by ingesting her, following the practice of his father Kronos, who swallowed his children. If the defensive strategy of Uranus is gross repression, and that of Kronos is coopting the new possibilities of life into the dominant attitude and then subjecting them to the solar ideals, the strategy of Zeus is perhaps even more thoroughgoing, for he attempts to incorporate the feminine herself, the anima, the mother of new possibilities. What may look like a bid for integration here is actually a defense aimed at robbing the unconscious of its creative, if also equally disruptive, potential.

This anxiety about authority and power on the part of the dominant archetypal pattern manifests itself as guilt. Even though the dominant pattern may in itself be considered amoral, solar conscience extracts values from it and holds them up to the ego dressed in the garb of a moral imperative. This is encountered routinely in psychotherapy. The patient is blocked in life, and instead of going through a transformative process that would allow for renewal and a new forward movement of development, the patient experiences acute guilt. Often therapy is begun by a person with the idea of patching things up; the patient wants to understand the blockage in order to overcome it and go on as before. Enter the Zeus type of solar conscience: it would integrate the unconscious resistances and challenges, build them somehow into the old dominant attitude, and even use the unconscious for its own ends. This usually fails, but guilt deepens, too, before a transformation can take place.

The implacable hostility of the "mothers" and of lunar conscience toward such persevering determination in the solar component is told in the oracles, always uttered by a mother, of impending dethronement. This oracular voice of nature adds a component to the clinical picture that screws up the pitch of ego anxiety and drives it into further extremes of scrupulosity and rigidity. Identity is threatened. In this type of hostile and adversarial relationship between solar and lunar conscience, the ego may enjoy a sense of "good conscience" insofar as it looks to solar conscience for support, but at the same time it begins to suffer from the uneasy sense of living in bad faith with the larger demands of life. Uneasiness about unlived life seeps into the frame. This sense of bad conscience toward life and individuation derives from the still, small voice of lunar conscience.

Only when lunar conscience gains enough strength to prohibit and block further movement within the dominant attitude is the ego forced to deal with it. But here, too, the Zeus aspect of solar conscience comes on with all the bristling hostility and brutal power at its command.

THE PROMETHEAN REBELLION

We can observe this play of forces in the myth of Prometheus. Although Prometheus is not himself directly a spokesman of lunar conscience, he has a close link to it, for according to Aeschylus he is the son of Themis. In the plays of Aeschylus, Prometheus takes the side of humans when Zeus wants to destroy the human race and create another sort of being. He plays the role of rebel in the script, defying the authority of Zeus by giving fire to humanity, cheating the gods of the best parts of the animal sacrifice, and waxing indignant in an attitude of self-righteousness when he is punished for his offenses. Over against Prometheus, Zeus plays the part of master and tyrant. He is unforgiving, vindictive, and brutally punitive.

It would not be inaccurate to say that typically a Zeus creates a Prometheus, although the opposite is also true: that is, strict enforcement of law constellates the outlaw, but the presence of an outlaw also drives authority to excesses of law enforcement. The hostile collision between Zeus and Prometheus becomes a spiral of worsening relations that exacerbates the tensions which already exist inherently between them. *Prometheus Bound* reaches an abysmal impasse when Zeus has Prometheus impaled on a mountain. Nailed to the Caucasus, he nevertheless proudly continues to hurl cries of outrage and threats of revenge toward Olympus.

The meaning of this powerful and dramatic classic confrontation between a rebellious Titan and the king of Olympus is anchored in the relationship between Prometheus and Themis. Aeschylus's play turns on the issue of justice and its relation to the power of the established order. As the play opens, Hephaestus, who is fixing Prometheus to the rock, comments: "Such is the reward you reap of your man-loving disposition. For you, a God, feared not the anger of the Gods, but gave honors to mortals beyond what was just" (28–30). This view represents the dominant judgment of Olympus, chiefly that of Zeus: human beings were not entitled to the gifts of Prometheus, for reasons of "justice." This is a reference to hubris and the question of human proportion vis-à-vis the gods.

Prometheus holds a different interpretation of what justice means. He sees the justice of Zeus as highly arbitrary power: "I know that he is savage," says Prometheus, "and his justice a thing he keeps by his own standard" (188–189). When we hear of what Prometheus did for the human race, we must grant that, from the human point of view, the Titan has a good case:

> As soon as he [i.e., Zeus] ascended the throne
> that was his father's, straightaway he assigned
> to the several Gods their several privileges
> and portioned out the power, but to the unhappy
> breed of mankind he gave no heed, intending
> to blot the race out and create a new.
> Against these plans none stood save I: I dared.

I rescued men from shattering destruction
that would have carried them to Hades's house . . .
(230–237)

In Prometheus's empathic reaction toward mortals, who are
despised and consigned to doom by the Olympian leader
Zeus, we see the action of lunar conscience seeking to save
the possibilities of life, for humanity, too, belongs to the cosmos. Empathy, reaching out to put the neglected and despised elements of life on their feet, keeping the cosmos
whole—these are the movements and gestures of lunar conscience.

Prometheus's description of his gifts to mankind lists
much that goes beyond the simple gift of fire and elucidates
its meaning:

But man's tribulation,
that I would have you hear—how I found them mindless
and gave them minds, made them masters of their wits.
I will tell you this not as reproaching man,
but to set forth the goodwill of my gifts.
First they had eyes but had no eyes to see,
and ears but heard not. Like shapes within a dream
they dragged through their long lives and muddled all,
haphazardly. They knew not how to build
brick houses to face the sun, nor work in wood.
They lived beneath the earth like swarming ants
in sunless caves. They had no certain mark
of winter nor of flowery spring nor summer,
with its crops, but did all this without intelligence
until it was I that showed them—yes, it was I—
stars' risings and their settings hard to judge.
And numbering as well, preeminent
of subtle devices, and letter combinations

> that hold all in memory, the Muses' mother skilled in craft,
> I found for them. (441–461)

The list goes on: the invention of drugs and medicine, seercraft and the interpretation of dreams and signs, the art of metallurgy . . . this compendium includes most of the arts and trades that are required for civilization. But the long list begins with a gift that represents the a priori of all human culture, namely ego-consciousness itself. Prometheus raised humans out of their bewilderment and dreamlike confusion, their witlessness and state of psychic possession, and made them the masters of their minds.

Yet it is precisely here that the problem lies: by putting humanity on its psychic feet, Prometheus in the same moment destroyed a prior relationship between humanity and the gods. This in turn promoted the delusion that humans are the supreme masters of their fates and brought about hubris, the cardinal sin of Greek culture. Humans would soon become like Prometheus and rebel against the gods of Olympus!

One further gift of Prometheus underscores his advocacy and support of delusion, too: he caused mortals to cease foreseeing their death and replaced the intuition of mortality with blind hope (250–252).

Prometheus behaves in many respects like an autonomous ego complex, going too far, overreaching, doing too much out of what might at first be laudable motives, full of self-righteous indignation, bursting with competitiveness, eager to supplant the old paternal authority with its own. While rooted in Themis and motivated originally by lunar conscience and the sense of justice, Promethean consciousness ends up with a pretense at rationality ("I am the master of my mind") while all the while living in the grossest self-deception and inflation with its delusions of mastery and its blind hope. An amount of this is surely needed by humans, but the proportions must be right. A sense of proportion, of what is fitting, is lacking in Promethean consciousness; the son of Themis, who represents precisely what is needed, a sense of justice and proportion, Prometheus ends up trapped in the posture of rebellion.

Psychopathy runs rampant in the umbrage of Prometheus. This is also, however, ironically where the humanistic, antireligion developments of the last several centuries have landed Western culture. What began as laudable and understandable rebellion against the authority of dogmatic religion and the absolute authority of the church has created in Western societies a psychological attitude of hubris and disrespect for the archetypal powers of the psyche. Conscience, both solar and lunar aspects, has been denied a place in the modern mentality, where only instrumental, so-called rational considerations carry weight. This is also true of most modern psychotherapy, where guilt and shame are treated as problems to be eliminated without examining the reasons for their presence. They are written off as symptomatic of lack of ego development. The truly mature person suffers no pangs of conscience, according to the modern creed.

It is worth noting that although Prometheus calls upon his mother Themis several times in the course of the play, she never once answers him. To Orestes, and especially to his bloodthirsty sister Electra, who represent solar conscience gone extreme in a furious outburst of murderous vindictiveness, Themis responds; but to Prometheus, who represents lunar conscience gone awry, she is silent, perhaps shamed. In the former case, Apollo furnishes moral support for murderous repression of the mother; in the latter case, Themis, as lunar conscience, undergirds the moral claims for defiance of the ruling father. If, in the first, we see the workings of conscience as repressor, in the second we see it ironically as a tacit promoter of psychopathy and lawlessness. In both cases, the disastrous events that follow develop out of a disharmonious relation between the spokespersons of solar and lunar conscience. At odds, they bring out the worst in each other.

The Promethean movement within the psyche begins in lunar conscience, when it perceives injustice and the repressed and neglected elements of the psychic cosmos and seeks to divert attention and care in their direction, with the intention of including them, of enlarging the ego-dominated configuration so as not to exclude the other parts. But when the solar aspect of conscience, with its insistence on authority and lawfulness, becomes hostile to this expansionistic, Eros-directed movement, the lunar impulse transforms into a combative force that enters into fierce competition, full of self-righteousness, self-pity, myopia, and psychopathic rebelliousness. The cry for justice becomes the battle cry of the repressed. Now lunar conscience overreaches and advocates for its children all too well and, in the end, manages to create an impasse of polarization and conflict. Law meets justice at the bridge and the swords are crossed.

This creates within the dominant configuration a tightly strung tension, in which the "lower" or "inferior" side feeds on delusions of grandeur and self-determination, ignores its relationship to the prevailing mores and traditions of society, and practices the arts of deceit and cunning. Here the movement of lunar conscience to dissolve the absolutisms of law and superegoic strictures and to soften their inflexibility—out of motives of compassion and empathy, and with an aim toward conserving the possibilities of life—can defeat its own ends by fostering a split and creating another line of rigidity. This is, for example, the rigidity of the authoritarian Marxist. It is as though lunar conscience has reversed itself.

ZEUS REVISITED

If Zeus, as an image of solar conscience, resembles his fore-fathers Kronos and Uranus in the palpable urgency to maintain power and authority and to promulgate opinions as laws which must be obeyed by all, he also differs from them in several significant ways. Most importantly, he does not repress or devour all of his children as they did. This speaks for less power-anxiety on his part and for a freer system of government. On Olympus, Zeus tolerates some debate and shows latitude on differing opinion. While retaining the prerogative of making final decisions himself, he meanwhile shows the flexibility of benevolent paternalism. Comes the ultimate challenge to his authority, however, as in the case of Prometheus or in his wars with the Titans, with the Giants, or with Typhon, he does not hesitate to pull out the bolt of lightning and to defend himself with all the weapons in his powerful arsenal.

Forewarned of a threat, Zeus ingests his first wife, the Titaness Metis, hoping by this to prevent the birth of his future rival. But this act of "integration" has an unforeseen consequence. One day Zeus gets a splitting headache and soon gives birth, through his head, to the fetus who was in the womb of his wife. This child who springs full-fledged from the head of her father is Athena, the consummate father's daughter. As the myth unfolds, Athena becomes a good companion to her father and one of his closest advisors.

This mythological story tells about the development of lunar conscience within the solar dominant. Athena, as Malamud points out in "The Amazon Problem," brings reflection: "she helps him [i.e., the hero] detach from the chaotic affect through reflection" (1971, p. 7). Athena introduces into the Zeus-dominated psyche an element of reflective interiority which softens the judgmental element in the solar

110

dominant. She functions, therefore, in a manner much like that of more classic representatives of lunar conscience, relativizing the absolutisms of the strict solar rule of law and, at the same time, expanding the interior of the dominant attitude to include figures who would otherwise be ignored or rejected. She performs this function in her role as protectress of cities and of certain heroes.

Unlike Zeus, Athena takes a lively interest in the affairs of humankind (Kerenyi 1988, p. 128). Moreover, it is Athena who intervenes in the tragic fate of Orestes and forces a solution to his plight:

> Orestes, once I saved you
> When I was arbiter on Ares' hill
> And broke the tie by voting in your favor.
> Now let it be the law that one who earns
> An evenly divided verdict wins
> His case.
> (Euripides, *Iphigenia in Taurus,* 1471–1475)

The mercy notes in this speech indicate the bias toward conserving the possibilities of life and bespeak Athena's inclination toward performing the function of lunar conscience in matters of justice.

If Athena has, in some respects, the role of lunar conscience within the Zeus-dominated world of Olympus, this function is heavily qualified by her unquestionable allegiance to her father. As Malamud observes, "Athena . . . belongs to her father, Zeus. The Parthenos repeatedly declares herself obedient to the father" (1971, p. 7). In *The Eumenides* Aeschylus has Athena say, as she passes judgment upon Orestes:

It is my task to render final judgment here.
This is a ballot for Orestes I shall cast.
There is no mother anywhere who gave me birth,
and, but for marriage, I am always for the male
with all my heart, and strongly on my father's side.
(734–738)

Athena represents, therefore, a rather pale version of lunar conscience, in that her claims and goals remain subservient to the solar dominant. Athena does not embody the far-reaching cosmic claims of lunar conscience, which in its ultimate outreach speaks for the *unus mundus* (the world as one). Rather, she represents an attempt from the solar side of conscience to incorporate some of the aspects of its lunar counterpart without accepting the ultimate challenges posed by the deeper level. Athena broadens the horizon of Zeus, interiorizes and softens the patriarchal cosmos, but does not fundamentally challenge the assumptions of Olympus. Instead she brings him support and introduces into his world of consciousness some strategic reflection and moments of interiority.

THE MARRIAGE OF ZEUS AND THEMIS

It is in the story of Zeus's marriage to Themis that we find the image of a possibly genuine conjunction of solar and lunar conscience. According to the Greek mythographers, Themis became the second wife of Zeus, after Metis and before Hera. When Zeus later married Hera, Themis took on the role of counselor. The Homeric hymn to Zeus places Themis beside the Olympian ruler:

I shall sing of Zeus, the best and the greatest of gods,
far-seeing, mighty, fulfiller of designs who confides

112

his tight-knit schemes to Themis as she sits leaning
upon him.
Have mercy, far-seeing Kronides, most glorious and
great!

Themis tempers the might of Zeus with her wisdom and with
the deep knowledge of and respect for the broad laws of nature that supersede even the will of almighty Zeus. A Titaness, her roots lie in the archaic world of pre-Olympian times
and extend outward to include a cosmic vision of the ultimate and final workings of the whole universe. As wife and
counselor to Zeus, she is also his mirror and mentor. In one
myth, she actually acts the role of nursemaid to baby Zeus,
already then teaching him respect for law and justice (cf.
Roscher).

There are parallels to the relationship of Zeus and
Themis in other mythologies. When Erda rises up out of the
earth in Wagner's Ring and counsels Wotan not to overstep
his limits, she is performing the function of Themis. In the
Bible, Sophia has a similar function in relation to Yahweh.
Jung comments extensively in his work *Answer to Job* on
this relationship, seeing in Sophia a "more or less hypo-
statized pneuma of feminine nature that existed before the
Creation" (1952, par. 609). Like Themis, this biblical figure
of feminine Wisdom reaches back to primordial times. Moreover, "as the cosmogonic Pneuma she pervades heaven and
earth and all created things" and represents God's eternal
justice (ibid., pars. 612, 614). As "the mother-beloved,"
Sophia is "a reflection of Ishtar, the pagan city goddess," and
as world-builder, she possesses a Maya character (ibid., pars.
612, 613). In Yahweh's treatment of Job, Jung sees the need
for an "anamnesis of Sophia" (ibid., par. 617), which reminds
us of Zeus's imbroglio with Prometheus, where Themis, too,
was apparently absent from the counsels of Olympus.

Most important of all, what Themis brings to Zeus, and Sophia to Yahweh, is an empathic and loving connection to humankind. On the absence of Eros in Yahweh's relation to his chosen people, his "bride," Israel, Jung comments:

> At the bottom of Yahweh's marriage with Israel is a perfectionist intention which excludes that kind of relatedness we know as "Eros." The lack of Eros, of relationship to values, is painfully apparent in the Book of Job: the paragon of all creation is not a man but a monster! Yahweh has no Eros, no relationship to man, but only to a purpose man must help him fulfill. . . . The faithfulness of his people becomes the more important to him the more he forgets Wisdom. (1952, pars. 621–622)

The attitude of Zeus toward humankind is quite different from that of Yahweh. Zeus is simply fundamentally uninterested and unconcerned. Sophia and Themis call for a thoroughgoing correction of this attitude.

The "perfectionist intention" is a characteristic feature of solar conscience, while the intention to maintain wholeness and to attain completeness signal the core values of lunar conscience. Neither one by itself alone is sufficient, for as Jung observed, "perfectionism always ends in a blind alley, while completeness by itself lacks selective values" (1952, par. 620). In the marriage of Themis and Zeus, we may be able to observe how these two radically different attitudes can join forces and work in tandem rather than in perpetual conflict.

In the context of our discussion, Zeus represents the solar aspect of conscience, the king. Solar conscience creates a sort of backbone in the archetypal pattern that governs and controls the ego-consciousness of the individual and the deep structure of society. This is the legal tradition of society and the element of lawfulness within the individual. This king factor is highly sensitive to challenges to its authority; it is easily turned to aggression against a violator of the law; it tends to fall into obsessive thinking, hair-splitting, legalistic ruminating; it censors and represses the influx of other possibilities as they intrude into consciousness and society.

The solar aspect of conscience both creates collectivity and enforces it. The collective consciousness of a group, with its norms of behavior and shared interpretations of experience and its common law, arises from the solar component of the archetype under which the group lives. Its internal enforcement in the individual takes place through the function of solar conscience. Through its insistence on lawfulness within the framework of the traditions of society, solar conscience contributes a high degree of stability and solidity to culture, and it creates and supports what is commonly called character in the individual. The shifty and selfish ego can be contained and held firmly in place to duty and can now, under the aegis of solar conscience, be counted upon to be tomorrow what it is today and was yesterday. It is the solar component of conscience that imbues archetypal configurations and social traditions with such immense durability and tenacity.

Complicating the picture, however, is the reality that no one lives entirely within one archetypal pattern. One has different roles to play in life, and each has it own typical patterns of attitude and behavior. Each also has the component of solar conscience. Thus, a businessman lives up to the standards of his professional life when he turns a profit, a husband when he provides for his family and remains faithful to his wife, a sportsman when he wins the contest without cheating on the rules of the game, and so on. Solar conscience presses for high performance within each of these various constellations and even provides overarching principles of achievement which can be applied to solve conflicts of duty when two or more roles or patterns collide. Solar conscience solves these conflicts of duty by a process of exclusion: one must choose one pattern over another (husband or lover, pacifist or militarist, capitalist businessman or socialist Christian), and the choice indicates in which archetype solar conscience is stronger. Solar conscience mines and refines the moral elements in each archetypal configuration.

Themis, the image of lunar conscience, moves also within each of the various archetypal patterns, but in a direction other than that of her solar counterpart. Lunar conscience tends to work more or less quietly in the background (except when angry, witness the Furies or Prometheus), undermining the absolutisms and certainties of Sol. She relativizes solar imperatives with an eye to the natural person and with the intention of including what has been neglected and left out. Where solar conscience would exclude one of a pair of conflicted parties and insist on an either/or decision, lunar conscience moves in the counter-direction by never failing to raise the nagging question about the excluded other. The value of lunar conscience is to include as much as possible.

Dionysius Andreas Freher (1649–1728) in his *Paradoxes Emblemata* pondered the meaning of the center and the circumference of a circle:

> The circumference consists of innumerable little points, answers fitly unto so many particular some-things, all distinguished and discernible from, and placed in number and order beside each other. But the center is only one individual point; as to its quantity not bigger than any of the rest, but as to qualities the most considerable of all, and in a sense so big as all the circumferential points taken all together; nay upon another account even infinitely bigger. For upon this

> only all the circumferential points do depend, being
> and having from that one all that they are and have.
> . . . (quoted in Hirst 1964, p. 186)

Applied to our discussion, this image of a circle with center
and circumference can provide a model for conceptualizing
the relation between the solar and lunar components of conscience. The various individual points on the circumference
of the circle, each with its particular space and discrete sin-
gularity, correspond to the various archetypal patterns
through which we move in the course of life, each with its
own ethical component that solar conscience upholds and
espouses, its own perfection, its own code of law. The effect
of the central point—lunar conscience, in our analogy—is to
join all of the discrete parts into a pattern of totality, without
eradicating any of the individual points. But as soon as one
of the circumferential points seeks to set itself up as the
dominant of all, the central point undermines it by joining it
to other points on the circumference of the circle. Thus it
works against the solar inclination that would distend the
circle outward or upward in the cause of perfection. Lunar
conscience wants the whole cosmos, not just one spot of perfect ground in it; the original person with all limbs intact,
not just a head or an eye. It speaks for the ethos of pluralism
while maintaining the connection of all the parts.

Lunar conscience creates conflicts of duty as well as
maintaining integrity by being unwilling to capitulate to a
solar "splitting" solution and by insisting instead on a both/
and position. Conflicts of duty have been solved traditionally
by consulting a book of moral casuistry, in which the hierarchies of responsibility are outlined, exceptions to rules are
given, and conditions for violation of norms set. At the end,
there is a solution. Such works are the creation of solar conscience. Sol has been busy working: starting from first prin-

ciples, duties are divided and subdivided according to their relative importance, their position in the hierarchy of values, their relative claims, their legal status. The aim of this enterprise is to salvage some modicum of moral perfection in a complex world. But take someone who follows such a moral system of codes and laws to the letter and look at the unconscious, at dreams, at fantasies, at the "psychopathology of everyday life" (slips of the tongue), and a different picture emerges of where libido is tending. St. Augustine thanked God he was not responsible for his dreams.

Searing ethical conflicts can arise out of the various competing interests within a solar conscience. Shall I be a good husband or a faithful lover? A responsible businessman or a moral citizen of the world? A dedicated patriot or a conscientious objector? Such conflicts can sometimes be solved by rational reflection, and in the end one solar ideal wins out over another. But equally wrenching conflicts arise when the unconscious is taken into account with moral seriousness. In that case, no matter which way you turn or what you decide, for Sol or for Luna, there is no moral satisfaction in the "solution," no sense of clear conscience, no "Well, at least I did the right thing" after the heady sacrifice. Something is always left out, some life unlived or some moral rule faulted. For Orestes, there was no perfect answer to the moral dilemma.

Because he took the voice of lunar conscience with such dead earnestness, Jung suffered from this type of conflict for most of his adult life. In his autobiography he wrote:

> The images of the unconscious place a great responsibility upon a man. Failure to understand them, or a shirking of ethical responsibility, deprives him of his wholeness and imposes a painful fragmentariness on his life. . . . (1961, p. 193)

118

But if ignoring these images "imposes a painful fragmentariness" on life, taking responsibility for them and bearing
the moral conflict which they arouse imposes a heavy burden as well. To this point, Jung spoke in a letter to his friend,
the Dominican priest Victor White:

> The more you know of it [i.e., the unconscious], the
> greater and heavier becomes your moral burden, be-
> cause the unconscious contents transform themselves
> into your individual tasks and duties as soon as they
> begin to become conscious. Do you want to increase
> loneliness and misunderstanding? Do you want to find
> more and more complications and increasing responsi-
> bilities? (1975, p. 172)

In these words we hear something of the moral suffering
Jung sustained as a result of enduring the conflict that re-
sides in the marriage of solar and lunar conscience.

If ignoring lunar conscience imposes a "painful fragmentariness" on life, what happens if we cling only to Luna,
ignore solar duties, and seek completeness by repressing solar conscience? This move is commonly known as "repressing the moral factor" or "swimming in the unconscious" because the element of lawfulness and obedience to social
norms is obviously missing. If this choice meets no visible or
conscious resistance from the side of Sol, due to excessive
weakness of attachment to father and to society, there still
remains the psychological problem of floating about bound-
lessly in a mass of possibilities and images. The structure is
not there. Luna can turn to lunatic. In the same letter as
quoted above, Jung comments on this:

> But it soon becomes dangerous to know more, because
> one does not learn at the same time how to balance it
> through a conscious equivalent. That is the mistake
> Aldous Huxley makes: he does not know that he is in

119

the role of the *Zauberlehrling,* who learned from his
master how to call the ghosts but did not know how to
get rid of them again. (Ibid., p. 173)

So from this type of avoidance and repression of the solar
element in conscience, one does not realize wholeness and
completeness but instead a surfeit of unconscious contents.

We come, then, to the rather obvious (by now) conclusion
that following the dictates of either lunar or solar conscience
to the exclusion of the other is both psychologically unacceptable and ethically reproachable. And yet, containing and
enduring the conflict imposed by taking both with moral seriousness exacts a high price, for the conflict has no definitive solution. The image of Zeus consulting Themis by his
side must not, therefore, be seen through rose-tinted glasses:
how wonderful, they've finally gotten it together, from now
on only sweet harmony. For between them passes wisdom,
and wisdom comes at a price and has, as the alchemists
noted, the taste not of sweetness but of salt.

In the image of Zeus conversing with Themis, we must
imagine a good deal of give and take. In most matters, Zeus
rules and decides, while Themis brings to the dominant attitude the softening, relativizing touch of a wider outlook.
Spirit and instinct are balanced in the counsels. This dialogue loosens the rigidities and certainties of solar conscience
without, however, necessarily rejecting or seeking to repress
it either. "Should I cross at the crosswalk?" "Yes, but not as
though you are obeying a law of nature." This loosening effect brought by Themis allows us to enact the norms of the
dominant pattern of self or culture without the compulsive-
ness that solar conscience by itself tends to inflict. In every
moral decision made by solar conscience, Themis has her
eye on what has been denied. And the stiffer and more per-
sistently rigid the mood of Zeus becomes, the sharper also

grows the resistance of Themis, so that one day the good citizen might find an irresistible compulsion to cross in the middle of the block and "Damn the crosswalk, I am a free man." As we saw earlier, this dynamic can readily become a Promethean phenomenon with its paranoid and psychopathic intensity, but only if the dialogue between Zeus and Themis breaks down.

If in most moral decisions of everyday life solar conscience leads the way and the lunar component adds a softening, relativizing touch, there also come crisis points in life where a major ethical choice is called for and the dialogue between Zeus and Themis must deepen. Zeus would preserve the pattern that has dominated until this moment, and his anxiety about power and authority adds intensity to his side of the argument. He wants to preserve the common law and tradition. Themis, on the other hand, has connections to the Fates, those powers which ultimately govern the natural order and which Zeus cannot control or shake from their determinations.

Here the conflict between Sol and Luna deepens, lawfulness and justice face off, and the competition of duties enters its most painful and acute phase. On the one hand, solar conscience insists on the old loyalties and the norms which have governed the ego until now: the old ego-ideal is polished up and held in the sun to reveal its golden splendor; the motives for movement and change are exposed in the grisliest light as nothing but egoistic power drive, infantile wish-fulfillment, inflation; the threat of guilt looms large, and not mild guilt—a few conscience pangs—but a *Weltuntergang-stimmung,* an atmosphere of worlds convulsing in agony. Lunar conscience, on the other hand, insists on the fatedness of this movement into the unknown: unless you lose your life, she will say, you will not find it; give up the power, let go of the ring of gold; the inferior must not be denied, in it there is not only evil but also the force of life, in the child not only infantilism but new energy and a future; after the convulsion new worlds will come into being.

To follow solar conscience in this dilemma would be to impose on life that "painful fragmentariness" of which Jung speaks, to shirk one's fate and thereafter to live as a hollow person within a world empty of passion and deeper meaning. To follow lunar conscience alone, on the other hand, would be to invite the punishments of guilt, the convulsions which accompany the death of an old life pattern, the uncertainty that what one is doing is "right." It was in such a dilemma that Luther stood at the Diet of Worms and, having made his choice for destiny, uttered the only words possible: *"Hier stehe Ich, Ich kann nicht anders, so helfe mir Gott"* ("Here I stand; I cannot do otherwise, so help me God").

The Japanese film *Rebellion* tells the story of a woman in eighteenth-century Japan who, having borne a son to the chief of the clan, was forced to leave the palace in favor of another concubine. Married off to a lesser man, the son of a nobleman, she soon fell deeply in love with him and he with her. Three years later, when it became apparent that her son would be heir to the chief, she was ordered to return to the palace and resume her place as head mistress.

The conflict provoked by this inhumane situation brings enormous pressures to bear upon her. If she returns, she will lose her beloved new husband; if she does not return, the chief will destroy her beloved and his entire family. Only her husband and her stepfather take the position that she should not go back to the chief; the rest of the family, looking out for themselves, of course, insist she should return.

In one scene the families, both hers and his, are gathered in a small room for a conference. She and her father sit facing one another, and the rest of the clan is gathered around them. Her father, who has had absolute mastery over her life until now, attempts to persuade her to return to the palace. She refuses, and he grows hot with indignation and points out that she is about to destroy them all. Stepmother and brother-in-law insist on the laws of filial piety: she must obey her father. He is her master.

Under this excruciating pressure, and with tears in her eyes, she says: "My father is my father, and I am I. And I cannot go back." And with this the fate of all is sealed.

When Themis takes the lead in the dialogue between solar and lunar aspects of conscience, the issues always hinge on questions of soul and fate. By his threats and his challenges, Zeus keeps the discussion honest; by exacting such an enormous penalty, he renders the sacrifice genuine, with no possibility of "clean conscience" and self-righteous moral superiority afterwards. Conscience as an archetype is also a *unio oppositorum,* a union of opposites, and as in all such unions there is enormous potential for tension and conflict. Within conscience, the antinomies, which I have designated as solar and lunar elements, never come peacefully to rest but forever struggle with each other, undermining, challenging, and relativizing all certainties and moral absolutisms. If conscience pushes us toward individuation, toward soul-making, it does so not without at the same time challenging the entire enterprise, and by this challenge it lends the quest its tone of honesty and serious humility.

REFERENCES

Aeschylus. *The Libation Bearers.* In *The Complete Greek Tragedies,* vol. 1. David Greene and Richmond Lattimore, eds. Chicago: University of Chicago Press, 1992.

_____. *Prometheus Bound.* In *The Complete Greek Tragedies,* vol. 1. Greene and Lattimore, eds. Chicago: University of Chicago Press, 1991.

Alsop, S. 1972. Commentary. *Newsweek,* October 15, 1972.

Athanassakis, A. N., trans. and ed. 1976. *The Homeric Hymns.* Baltimore: Johns Hopkins University Press.

Bachofen, J. J. 1954. *Myth, Religion, and Mother Right.* Princeton, N.J.: Princeton University Press.

Bonnet, H. 1952. *Reallexikon der aegyptischen Religionsgeschichte.* Berlin.

Brandon, S. G. F. 1967. *The Judgment of the Dead.* New York: Charles Scribner's Sons.

Brown, Norman O. 1966. *Love's Body.* New York: Vintage.

Budge, E. A. 1969. *The Gods of the Egyptians,* vol. 1. New York: Dover.

Cirlot, J. E. 1991. *A Dictionary of Symbols.* New York: Dorset Press.

Eliade, M. 1963. *Myth and Reality.* New York: Harper and Row.

Euripides. *Iphigenia in Taurus.* In *The Complete Greek Tragedies,* vol. 3. Greene and Lattimore, eds. Chicago: University of Chicago Press, 1992.

Farnell, L. R. 1907. *The Cults of the Greek States.* Oxford: Oxford University Press.

Grinnell, R. 1973. *The Alchemical Process in a Modern Woman.* Dallas: Spring Publications.

Guntrip, H. 1989. *Schizoid Problems, Object Relations and the Self.* New York: International Universities Press.

Hamilton, E., and H. Cairns, eds. 1961. *The Collected Works of Plato.* New York: Pantheon.

Harrison, J. 1912. *Themis.* Cambridge: Cambridge University Press.

Hesiod. *Theogony.* In *Hesiod.* Richmond Lattimore, trans. Ann Arbor, Mich.: University of Michigan Press, 1973.

Hesse, H. 1919. *Demian*. London: Paladin Grafton Books, 1989.

Hillman, J. 1970. On senex consciousness. *Spring*. Dallas: Spring Publications.

Hirst, D. 1964. *Hidden Riches*. London.

Holt, D. 1973. Jung and Marx. In *Spring*. Dallas: Spring Publications.

Ibsen, H. 1965. *The Complete Major Prose Plays*. Rolf Fjelde, trans. New York: Times Mirror.

Ions, V. 1965. *Egyptian Mythology*. New York: Paul Hamlyn.

Jacobsohn, H. 1968. The conversation of the world-weary man with his soul. In *Timeless Documents of the Soul*. Evanston, Ill.: Northwestern University Press.

Jung, C. G. 1931. Problems of modern psychotherapy. In *CW* 16:53–75. Princeton, N.J.: Princeton University Press, 1954.

_____. 1937. Psychological factors determining human behavior. In *CW* 8114–125. Princeton, N.J.: Princeton University Press.

_____. 1948. The spirit Mercurius. In *CW* 13:191–250. Princeton, N.J.: Princeton University Press, 1967.

_____. 1950. A study in the process of individuation. In *CW* 9i:290–354. Princeton, N.J.: Princeton University Press, 1969.

_____. 1952. *Answer to Job.* In *CW* 11:355–472. Princeton, N.J.: Princeton University Press, 1969.

_____. 1954. Transformation symbolism in the Mass. In *CW* 11:201–296. Princeton, N.J.: Princeton University Press, 1958.

_____. 1955–1956. *Mysterium Coniunctionis. CW,* vol. 14. Princeton, N.J.: Princeton University Press, 1963.

_____. 1957. Commentary on "The Secret of the Golden Flower." In *CW* 13:1–56. Princeton, N.J.: Princeton University Press, 1967.

_____. 1958. A psychological view of conscience. In *CW* 10:437–455. Princeton, N.J.: Princeton University Press, 1964.

_____. 1961. *Memories, Dreams, Reflections.* New York: Random House.

_____. 1975. *Letters,* vol. 2. Princeton, N.J.: Princeton University Press.

◆ REFERENCES ◆

Kerenyi, K. 1988. *The Gods of the Greeks.* New York: Thames and Hudson.

Kierkegaard, S. 1961. *Purity of Heart Is to Will One Thing.* London: Fontana Books.

Kohlberg, L. 1973. Continuities in childhood and adult moral development revisited. In *Life-Span Developmental Psychology,* P. B. Baltes and K. W. Schaie, eds. New York: Academic Press, 1973.

Malamud, R. 1971. The Amazon problem. In *Spring.* Dallas: Spring Publications, 1971.

Neumann, E. 1954. *The Origins and History of Consciousness.* New York: Pantheon Books.

_____. 1969. *Depth Psychology and a New Ethic.* New York: G. P. Putnam's Sons.

_____. 1974. *The Great Mother.* Princeton, N.J.: Princeton University Press.

Rado, S. 1960. Rage, violence and conscience. In *Comprehensive Psychiatry* 1(6):327–330.

Roscher, W. H. 1924–1937. *Ausfuehrliches Lexikon der griechischen und roemischen Mythologie.* Leipzig: Teubner.

Scholl, R. 1970. *Das Gewissen des Kindes.* Stuttgart.

Schwartz-Salant, N. 1989. *The Borderline Personality: Vision and Healing.* Wilmette, Ill.: Chiron Publications.

Stein, M. 1985. *Jung's Treatment of Christianity.* Wilmette, Ill.: Chiron Publications.

Strauss-Kloebe, S. 1934. *Ueber die psychologische Bedeutung des astrologischen Symbols.* In *Eranos Jahrbuch* 1934.

von Franz, M.-L. 1981. *Puer Aeternus.* Santa Monica: Sigo Press.

von Monakow, C. 1950. *Gehirn und Gewissen* [Brain and Conscience]. Zurich.

Zimmer, H. 1951. *Philosophies of India.* Princeton, N.J.: Princeton University Press.

INDEX

active imagination, 79, 83, 87
adolescence, 30-31, 75
Adrasteia, 73-74
Aeschylus, 58, 61, 63, 69, 104-105,
    111
aggression, 11-12, 115
alchemy, 21, 72
ambivalence, 2-3
Ammut, 85
anima, 7, 48, 103
animus, 7, 82
anxiety, 25, 27-28, 30, 34, 40, 64,
    99-100, 103, 121
    abandonment, 28, 33
    castration, 49
    separation, 34
Aphrodite, 9-10
Apollo, 57-59, 61, 66, 69-71, 77, 93,
    108
archetype, 5, 7, 13, 16, 88, 92, 100,
    102, 115-116, 123
    moral, 66
    of conscience, 28
    of the Great Mother, 39, 62
    of the unconscious, 21
    theory of, 12
Ares, 74, 85
Artemis, 9-10, 57, 88-89, 93-94
astrology, 39
Athena, 90, 93, 110-112
authority, 11, 13, 17-18, 98-104,
    107-110, 115, 121
    collective, 14
autism, 33

Bachofen, J. J., 19, 59-61, 66-68,
    91, 94
Bible, 32, 113
Bonnet, H., 85
borderline personality disorder, 56,
    61
Brandon, S. G., 84-86
Brown, N. O., 11
Budge, E. A., 84-85, 87

case examples, 23-24, 48-50, 80-83
Christ, 21
Christian doctrine, vs. Gnostic, 72
Cirlot, J. E., 78
collective attitude, 58
collective consciousness,13, 31, 53,
    61, 73, 88, 115
    see also authority, collective;
    culture; society
complex, 5-7, 15, 19, 63, 96, 99, 101
    ego, 29, 107
    mother, 80-81
confession, 23, 25-26
crime, 26, 34, 45, 56, 92-94, 98
culture, 17, 24, 27-28, 31-32, 36, 40,
    48, 56, 59, 67, 73, 79, 89, 95, 99,
    107, 115, 120
    see also tradition
    Greek, 64, 107
    hippy, 101
    Western, 72, 88, 108
Curie, M., 3
Cybele, 73

death, 19, 64, 69, 82, 107
Delphi, 57, 69-70, 72, 86, 93
Demeter, 69
depression, 21
Devil (devil), 8-9
dharma, 95
Dike, 19, 63, 76-79, 83-84, 87, 95
Diodorus, 48
Dostoevsky, F., 6
dreams, 17, 19, 48-49, 61, 65, 68, 70-
    71, 77, 79-84, 86, 96, 107, 118
duty, 115-117, 119, 121

ego, vii, 2-3, 5-7, 9-16, 18, 21-22, 25-
    26, 28-37, 39-40, 43, 46, 48, 51,
    56, 60-63, 65-66, 75, 78-79, 82-83,
    86-87, 89, 97-100, 102-104, 108,
    115, 121
    dream, 50
ego-consciousness, 18, 41, 46-47, 79,
    87, 101, 107, 114

131